'The Most Fruitful Experiment'

‘The Most Fruitful Experiment’

The Montgomery County Recreation Association, 1919-2019

Jennifer Lane

MCRA

Published by: Montgomeryshire County Regeneration Association, Plas Dolerw, Milford Road, Newtown, Powys SY16 2EH, Wales

ISBN: 978-1-9161987-0-8

ACKNOWLEDGMENTS

First of all, I would like to express my thanks to the Montgomeryshire Community Regeneration Association for commissioning this short history of the MCRA and for giving me full access to their wonderful collection of the Association's records.

I have received valuable assistance from members and staff of the MCRA. I am particularly grateful to David Hall, who not only set the brief for this centenary history but also provided additional material and clarifications. Also, I would like to thank Clair Stevens for her hospitality and for making access to the extensive materials as easy as possible, and to Angela Williams for assisting with my last-minute enquiries. I would also like to thank Susan Hamer for advice on locating records of the Gwendoline and Margaret Davies Charities.

In addition to individuals connected with the MCRA, I am grateful to the staff of the National Library of Wales and of Powys Archives for their valuable assistance in arranging access to supporting documents and to the National Library of Wales for its freely available access to digitized newspapers through the British Newspapers Archive. Finally, I am immensely grateful to Paul O'Leary for his plentiful advice and the patience he has shown throughout.

CONTENTS

INTRODUCTION **1**

1: BEGINNINGS, 1919 .... **5**

Formation of the Association 5

Aims and Objects 9

Influences, Context and People 11

2: INTO ACTION, 1919-20 .... **17**

Early Activity 19

Planning Ahead 21

Cinema 21

Sports Clubs and Leagues 23

County Sports Day 27

Aftermath 32

3: EXPANSION, ACHIEVEMENTS AND CHALLENGES, 1920-22 .... **36**

Local Associations 37

Grounds 40

Village Institutes 42

Funding Institutes 48

Music 52

The Festival 55

Infrastructure and Economic Context 62

4: RESCUE AND CONSOLIDATION, 1924-39 .... **64**

The Impact of Reorganization 66

Music 68

Institutes, Centre and Locality 73

Recreation Grounds and Funding 77

Co-operation, Networks and the Voluntary System 80

The Gregynog Network 85

Transition 87
5: WAR AND MODERNIZATION, 1939-82 89
The War and its Aftermath 90
The End of an Era 92
A New Era and a New Generation 93
The Impact of the Modernizing State 99
Lost Property: Community House and the Pavilion 101
Seeking a New Role 106
6: ART AND THE COMMUNITY, 1967-2019 108
Antecedents: Welshpool and Newtown 109
The Memorial Gallery 110
Oriel 31 at the Memorial Galley 116
The Memorial Gallery at Risk: The Mid-Wales Arts Centre 120
A New Sense of Purpose: Art and Community 122
Community, Art and Compromise 126
Oriel Davies Gallery 130
CONCLUSIONS 134
APPENDICES 138
Appendix I: Extract from the 'Rules of the Association' 138
Appendix II: The Davies family financial contribution 142
Appendix III: Village Institutes erected by the MCRA 149
Appendix IV: People – Presidents, Officers and Others 152
Notes 158

TIMELINE

1919	Formation of the Montgomery County Recreation Association, Newtown, 22 July.
	Large donations were made by the Davies family in this and following years.
1920	County Sports Day organised by the MCRA, Newtown, 17 July.
	First army hut erected as a village institute in Abermule, 11 November.
	The MCRA appointed the first County Music Organizer for Montgomeryshire.
1921	The first County Music Festival, and opening of the County Pavilion, held on 21 July.
	The County Recreation Ground was purchased for the MCRA by David Davies.
1926	Financial rescue of the MCRA by David, Gwendoline and Margaret Davies.
1931	Sale of the County Recreation Ground to Newtown and Llanllwchaiarn Urban District Council.
1931-32	Launch of the Montgomery Rural Community Council by MCRA officers and members.
1939	The MCRA appointed its first Rural Industries organizer.
1944	Death of Lord Davies on 16 June.
1950	The MCRA adopted a new constitution, as a company limited by guarantee.
1967	The Davies Memorial Gallery was opened by Sir Ben Bowen Thomas. It was funded by the Gwendoline and Margaret Davies charities.

1968	The MCRA ceased to run the Rural Industries initiative following a change in government policy.
1974	Sale of the County Pavilion to Newtown and Llanllwchaiairn Urban District Council.
	Sale of Community House to the Mid Wales Development Corporation.
1975	Formation of Powys Rural Council; MCRA lost all rural council functions.
	Reorganisation of local government created Powys County Council.
1982	The Music Festival became independent of the MCRA and responsibility for it was passed to Theatr Hafren.
1985	Oriel 31 moved into the Davies Memorial Gallery.
2000	The MCRA purchased Plas Dolerw, Newtown, with funding from the Gwendoline and Margaret Davies charities, the Tudor Trust and Powys County Council.
2002	The MCRA moved into Plas Dolerw, after refurbishment which was funded by the Community Fund and others.
	The Davies Memorial Gallery was closed for refurbishments, which were funded by the Arts Council for Wales, the Gwendoline and Margaret Davies charities, Powys County Council, and the Wales Tourist Board.
2005	Opening of the completed Oriel Davies Gallery by Lembit Opik, MP.
2007	The MCRA's name was changed to the Montgomeryshire Community Regeneration Association.
2016	Newtown Textile Museum became a sub-committee of the MCRA.

INTRODUCTION

This centenary history was commissioned by the MCRA in January 2019.

It begins with an account of the MCRA's origins in 1919 as the Montgomery County Recreation Association, a name it retained for almost ninety years. The first three chapters cover the short, but exceptionally active, formative years between 1919 and 1926, when lasting achievements and short-lived experiments followed in rapid succession. The first of these chapters explores the ideas behind the MCRA's formation and the role of David Davies in establishing it. The second chapter focuses on the MCRA's experiments with sports and entertainments, which were intended to bear fruit quickly, while the third chapter primarily investigates a programme of work that took a little longer to put into operation but produced such long-standing achievements as the County Music Festival and the creation of a network of village institutes.

Chapters four and five deal with two longer periods of time, together covering more than fifty years. This long period of relatively stable daily activity begins and ends with transitional phases, as the MCRA changed the nature of its activity in response to financial circumstances and external forces. The final chapter overlaps chronologically with chapter five, in order to allow a coherent account of the origins and development of Oriel Davies Gallery and its relationship to the MCRA's commitment to community work. There is supporting information about the Davies family funding, the number of village institutes that were constructed, and some key individuals in the appendices.

The study has been compiled mainly from the MCRA's large collection of yet-to-be archived original documents dating from its earliest days. It is a very impressive collection of material, but the documentation is more comprehensive in some periods than in others. Financial records are much less complete than records of minutes of meetings. It is a pity that the accounts for the first two years are not in the surviving archives, for instance, as they would have added more certainty to some aspects of the discussion in the early chapters. Some early record books appear to have been re-used in the Second World War, while mid-century records are on the whole less informative than earlier and later material. This archive has been supplemented by limited reference to contemporaneous newspaper accounts and, in the later period, references to the private papers of related parties that have been deposited in the National Library of Wales.

Owing to limitations of time and space, it has not been possible to discuss more than a few of the individuals who took part in the Association throughout its history, which has the unfortunate effect of making it appear even more male-dominated than necessary. There were few women, but there were some; generally, one or two were at least theoretically members of the governing body of the time and more were involved in the music festival throughout its history as part of the MCRA.

Finally, the MCRA dealt with many other bodies, and during the course of one hundred years those that continued to exist have changed their names, often more than once. To avoid the discussion being overwhelmed by acronyms and institutional family trees, this study refers as much as possible to all other bodies in generic form, e.g. 'county council' refers to whichever of the three different county councils was in force at the time in question. The MCRA, which has also changed its name and its constitution in the period covered, is referred to as the Association, the County Association or the MCRA, depending on context.

Parliamentary, county and district boundaries after 1917

This map was prepared by the Boundary Commission in 1917 and is reproduced under a creative commons public licence http://creativecommons.org/licenses/by/4.0/. The original has been cropped and the heading and reference presented separately. The original may be found at (http://www.VisionofBritain.org.uk).

1: BEGINNINGS, 1919

Much will be heard of the Recreation Association of the County of Montgomery. Pioneers in rural areas all over the four kingdoms will turn to Montgomery, as housing pioneers went for inspiration to Bourneville and Port Sunlight. For in Montgomeryshire is being carried out the most fruitful experiment yet attempted to bring some brightness into the drab monotonous existence of those who work upon the land.

Revd Gwilym Davies, 1920[1]

Formation of the Association

An evening in the Scala Theatre in Newtown would normally have attracted a paragraph or two in the local press at most in the early twentieth century. However, the event on Tuesday evening, 22 July 1919, generated much more excitement. In the weeks and months that followed, newspapers in the county and beyond, as well as the noted periodical *Welsh Outlook*, published column after column of coverage about the meeting. All discussed in laudatory terms the outcome of a public meeting attended by a crowd of notable and civic-minded people from across Montgomeryshire. The *Montgomery County Times* reported that 'sportsmen from all over the County' were present, but not all were there to foster sport alone, and indeed not all were men.[2] They came to hear and give support to a proposal that encompassed recreation 'in its widest and most liberal sense', from sports and pastimes to music and other aspects of intellectual culture.[3] This was the inauguration of the Montgomery County Recreation Association.

The proposal was the brainchild of Major David Davies MP, and the meeting was convened on his behalf by Captain J. Glynn Jones. Both local newspapers (The *County Times* and the *Montgomeryshire Express and Radnor Times*) reported a number of speeches in support of the idea. Mr Richard Jones, Chair of the County Council, expressed the view that the existing array of clubs, each of which worked in their own way, needed organizing and proper authority. He explained that this mattered because they were 'living in times when everyone seemed to be working at a high pressure and the people needed some kind of organised recreation'.[4]

It was Major W. J. Burdon-Evans, a secretary to Major Davies, who moved that the County Association be formed. His argument in favour of doing so is a reminder of the impact of the Great War, which had finished less than a year earlier. He mentioned the need for the population to be in a good physical condition, a view derived from statements by the army medical boards that recruited during the recent war, stating the need for A1 men, not C3 men. He referred to the potential effects of post-war reconstruction on the county: in the future there would be a greater tendency for men to take up employment in the country (through a government programme of land reform and small holdings). Retaining the population in rural areas was also a concern: it was up to them to make rural life more attractive, said Burdon-Evans, if they were to combat excessive migration from the villages to the towns. Finally, he noted the tendency for ordinary people to have longer leisure hours, which needed to be spent in a way that was both congenial to them and 'conducive to good results'.[5]

The war was also in the mind of the seconder, Canon C. M. Woosnam. He was thankful that so excellent a proposal had arisen out of the war. Although he agreed that matters of physique had been shown to be important by the war – citing that tenet of public education *mens sana in corpore sano* (a healthy mind in a healthy body) – his primary focus was on the moral benefit of the right sort of recreation. He expressed a hope that the Association would bring great moral benefit to the community by diverting the minds of young people.

Burdon-Evans explained that the proposers were 'primarily out to create enthusiasm', especially in the winter months when it was most needed. He discussed a range of possible activities, with particular emphasis on the provision of a travelling cinema, that could be carried out by an energetic and enthusiastic organization.

Then there were the practicalities. Major David Davies, he assured the meeting, was prepared to do a great deal for them. Much was made of Davies's promise to place the services of Captain Glynn Jones at the disposal of the association as organizer. In fact, his qualifications for the role were reported not so much with approval as with glee.

This recently demobilized officer, not yet thirty years of age, had 'a splendid military record, a host of very creditable athletic achievements to his credit', and he had already done much of the 'pioneer spadework in connection with the scheme'. Burdon-Evans asserted that Glynn Jones 'knew all there was to know about sport and had made a reputation for himself as a hustler and an athlete' in the army; by hustling he had been able to get things done and could do so again.[6] Perhaps of equal interest to the assembly in the Scala theatre was the news that Major Davies promised to give them the freehold of the recreation ground at Llandinam, as well as to provide them with central offices, and to place at their disposal his pack of beagles. In addition, he was prepared to give a substantial donation to their funds.[7] All this was very well received by those present at the meeting, and the Major's proposal was carried unanimously. The *Montgomeryshire Express* reported the establishment of the Association in auspicious terms:

> *The one epoch-making event of the past week has been the inauguration of the proposed*

County Recreation Association ... The County Member [David Davies] has launched many an ameliorative project, but none we think capable of more widespread or far-reaching results than the County Recreation Association.[8]

Aims and Objects

Those present in the inaugural meeting had before them a printed statement of the proposed objects and scope of the Association. The *Montgomeryshire Express* had seen the statement in advance, so it could hail the proposal enthusiastically as one that all those interested in outdoor and indoor recreation would 'scan with anticipatory delight'.[9] Recreation was defined in broad terms. It is clear from reports in both of the local newspapers that the proposal listed an illustrative range of activities (its scope) and the ways in which the Association would stimulate such activity (its scheme of work). For example, fifteen outdoor sports – from football and hockey to cycling and hunting – were mentioned in the press reports, along with the Boy Scouts and Girl Guides. The indoor recreations mentioned were fewer in number and included some indoor sports – billiards and badminton – but reports mainly focused on the cultural activities of music, drama and eisteddfodau, on lectures and debating societies, and on the travelling cinema that was so strongly emphasized in Burdon-Evans's presentation.[10]

M.C.R.A.—3a.

MONTGOMERY

County Recreation Association.

= Rules =

OF THE

County Association.

PRICE:—FOUR PENCE.

"Express" Printing Works, Newtown.

The Rules, price four pence.

A fuller guide to the overall objects and the scheme of work that was envisaged can be found in the Association rule book, published the following year.[11] The emphasis on 'recreation in its widest and most liberal sense' illustrated the same concerns that had been raised at the inaugural meeting: these were physical activity, moral tone and the proper use of leisure. The preamble to the rule book includes objectives such as providing village halls, public recreation grounds and playing fields; promotion of 'the moral, mental, and physical training and culture of the inhabitants', improving 'the condition of the working and poorer classes and [providing] them with the means of healthy recreation in their leisure time'.[12] It also gave an indication of how it was all to be arranged. Local recreation associations would be set up, co-operation with other societies and voluntary organizations would be necessary, and the new Association would co-ordinate everything.

Influences, Context and People

The driving force behind the formation of the scheme, Major David Davies, was not present at the public meeting that led to the formation of the County Association, nor was he present at its subsequent meetings. His influence, on the other hand, was always present, not simply as the funder of many of its practical activities, and employer of its secretary, but also in his determination to promote the ideas it embodied. Much later, the MCRA explained that some of those ideas originated in his army days:

> *During the war of 1914-18, our Founder was the Officer Commanding the 14th Battalion, Royal Welsh Fusiliers. During his period of service he came into contact with many officers who proved enthusiastic and efficient men. Many subjects were discussed including the rehabilitation of service men upon demobilisation. The result of those discussions was that at least four of those officers were*

> *found employment, two of them actually concerned with the formation of the Association, one as Chairman, and the other, Capt. Glyn Jones, O.B.E., M.C., as the first Secretary of the organisation early in 1919.*[13]

The idea of a county-wide organization of recreational activity had been in Davies' mind much earlier, however, in response to his concerns about rural depopulation in rural Montgomeryshire. As 'D. D.' wrote in *Llandinam* magazine as early as 1901, people left rural areas for better wages, opportunity, and simply for more to do.

> *They complain that the country is too dull for them. What remedy is to be found which will counteract this craving for excitement? The only suggestion which we have to make is that our village games and sports, our amusements and recreations, both literary and athletic, should be better organized, more systematically carried out, and that the employers should as often as possible, especially during times of inactivity ... allow their labourers to engage in wholesome recreation and enjoyment. We do not see why debating societies, football and cricket clubs, should not be organised on a County basis, with a central Administrative Board, consisting of representatives elected by the*

> *different village clubs. Such a Board would be able to supervise and make uniform rules for different competitions, and would foster at the same time a spirit of 'esprit de corps' in the different clubs which it represented.*[14]

In 1901, Davies (fresh from his undergraduate studies at Cambridge) expressed alarm at the consistency and degree of rural depopulation in Montgomeryshire. The scale of the problem locally differed from the picture across the country only in being more serious. He drew attention to the local impact of this, pointing out that the population of Llandinam parish had fallen in every census, except for 1871, while the population of Montgomeryshire recorded by the 1901 census had fallen by over 3,000. His key concern was that this level of depopulation imperilled the future of agriculture, such that 'the farmer knows not where to look for the necessary labour'.[15] This concern was widely shared, and one that the young Davies suggested could be addressed by taking action to counter each of the underlying reasons for depopulation. These actions included promoting training in agricultural science, while he hinted at land or tenancy reform, and concluded with his ideas for recreation. In this scheme of ideas, recreation and leisure were fundamental to retaining the viability of agriculture.

By 1901 Davies may well have been aware of new interpretations of leisure, generated through the work of major social thinkers of the time. A school of thought called 'social idealism' was dominant in British universities, and its ideas were distinguished by its supporters' emphasis on taking concrete action. In his study of approaches to leisure in this period, Robert Snape argues that '[t]he free time of British citizens was increasingly seen as a sphere of social citizenship and community-building. Through major social thinkers, including William Morris, Thomas Hill Green, Bernard Bosanquet and John Hobson, leisure and voluntarism were theorized in terms of the good society'.[16] Voluntary action was redefined as a moral responsibility rather than an act of kindness, no longer simply good works by the wealthy, but a commitment to improving society. This optimistic approach to the possibilities of widespread leisure is evident in David Davies' early views and it was just as evident in the widely-reported enthusiasm for the foundation of the MCRA in 1919.

In Montgomeryshire, as elsewhere, it took the urgency of post-war reconstruction to turn social concern into organization. David Davies was instrumental in putting the county in the forefront of the revived interest in what was now called 'social work'. As a Member of Parliament with excellent connections, it is likely that he was in touch with those behind a range of organizations and movements that were formed, or events that gained impetus, immediately after the war. One example of this is the National Conference on the Leisure of the People, held in Liverpool in November 1919, which explored themes that were particularly close to the concerns that motivated the MCRA. It is not clear whether the Association was formally represented at the Liverpool conference, but its founders were certainly in contact with Dr Walford Davies, who spoke there.

A few months later, at David Davies' suggestion, Captain Jones represented the MCRA at a follow-up conference that resolved to set up a central (national) committee or council representing 'societies concerned with the right use of leisure'. In the interests of sharing good practice and solving problems it called for *The Times* to publish a social work supplement, as it already did for education.[17] This initiative appears to be connected to the beginnings of the National Council of Social Service, with which the MCRA would have a long association. Montgomeryshire was among the pioneers of the new social work, but it was not a lone voice.

Eighteen years after he floated the idea of county-based recreation in the *Llandinam* magazine, the experience of war and the uncertain progress of reconstruction seem to have made David Davies even more convinced that it was needed. By now his political connections and experience, added to the force of his proposal, gave the new County Association access to influential people and organizations. His support allowed all involved in the venture to be confident that much could be achieved, and his substantial financial contributions were fundamental to its early successes. All these factors were acknowledged at the first business meeting of the newly-formed MCRA in September 1919, when a 'hearty vote of thanks was passed to Major David Davies for his great generosity and forethought in bringing forward this scheme which was going to be of so much benefit to the County'.[18]

2: INTO ACTION, 1919-20

The MCRA was set up as a voluntary movement. Its members all gave their time unpaid, and the intention was to foster voluntary work in localities throughout the county. To get started, however, it relied heavily on the work of full-time staff, beginning with the first secretary, Captain J. Glynn Jones, who was seconded from David Davies' personal staff. His energetic presence allowed the MCRA, in its first few months, to begin work on plans for a wide range of activities that ran in parallel. Some of these could be up and running in a few months, while others would by their nature take longer to show results. Some were envisaged as recurrent activity, others as one-off projects. There were ambitious plans for establishing infrastructure for sporting and community activities. This was intended to rectify the shortage of recreation grounds and village institutes in the county. Doing this would take time, without considering the activities that were to take place in these facilities, but without it many other ideas would be difficult to implement in the long term. Keeping up enthusiasm in the short term also called for more immediately visible results: these included plans for arranging a travelling cinema, organizing lectures and setting up competitive leagues in a variety of sports.

With these ambitions in view, it soon became necessary to advertise for an assistant to Captain Jones. Early in 1920 the Association advertised for an Assistant

Secretary with business experience. The appointment stirred up a vehement storm of protest from members of an organization called the Comrades of the Great War, and the matter was pursued through the press for weeks afterwards. The Comrades were outraged that the Association's choice, O. D. S. Taylor, was not an ex-serviceman. The Montgomeryshire Divisional Council of the Comrades, and four of its local branches, wrote to the Association and the press to protest against the appointment of a civilian. So did Canon Woosnam, an early supporter of the MCRA. They were not mollified at all by the Association's response, which was to send the Divisional Council a full account of the decision process. The shortlisting panel had agreed that all other things being equal it would give preference to ex-servicemen; the interview panel included at least two ex-servicemen, and the votes cast were recorded.[1] This simply fuelled another round of protests through the press, especially in the *County Times*, this time taking aim at both the Association and those Comrades who were on the appointment panel. After a honeymoon period of widespread public support, this was the Association's first experience of outright hostility. The episode threatened the high ideals of co-operation that the MCRA had set out at the start. There was nothing the Association could do to stem the immediate tide of criticism other than refuse to rescind its decision[2] and get on with organizing its growing programme of activities.

Early Activity

Examples of activities that could be arranged quickly by the secretary included two very different programmes: the first was a touring lecture series and the second a programme of beagle meets, making use of David Davies' pack of beagles. The beagles were the easiest to arrange, as Davies had offered to make his existing pack available to the Association at the outset. This activity proved to be popular, especially when in 1920 he handed over the running of his beagles pack to the MCRA. After this, a Foot Beagle Club was formed and it took on the organization of meets. These continued to be popular in successive years, being regularly reported in the press and attracting anything from ten to 250 people.[3] By contrast, the lecture programme called for suitable lecturers and topics to be identified and contacted, and so needed more central organization. However, lectures could be arranged through the YMCA, so by the autumn of 1919 the secretary was able to draw up an experimental programme, listing five lecturers and topics.

The actual arrangements did not quite follow the plan, but the first lecture series was more successful than anticipated. The first lecture was held in four localities (Chirbury, Carno, Caersws and Cemmaes), although these were not the ones envisaged in the programme. The lecture was delivered by Miss Mary Procter, a noted astronomer and meteorologist, whose subject was 'The

Romance of Starland'. It went well: she attracted 200 people in Cemmaes, despite heavy rain. Attendance in the other three locations was equally impressive, ranging from 140 to 220, with the secretary reporting enthusiastic responses from those attending in spite of adverse weather. In all, thirty-five lectures were arranged between January and March 1920.[4] The surviving records do not list all of the lectures given, but the local press reported lectures in localities all over the county, although without supplying attendance figures. As intended, this was to become a recurrent activity in the following years, and for the remainder of the decade the Association persisted with its efforts to encourage local associations to host more lectures, as well as promoting training and correspondence classes, especially in co-operation with the Workers' Educational Association and the University of Wales extension services.

Other actions that took place in the early months were preparatory. One of the first was obtaining trophies and prizes, and persuading people to pay for them. In December 1919, Miss Heap was asked to obtain a sponsor for a Ladies' Hockey Shield,[5] which she duly did, the Shield being paid for by Mrs Price-Davies. By the following spring, the Association had a full complement of gold and silver medals for football leagues, as well as engraved cups for senior and junior cricket, football, and brass bands, all paid for by Major Davies and Captain Naylor.[6] This impressive array of silverware demonstrated an intention to co-ordinate sporting competition in the county, but it also meant progress could be reported in the press at a time when there would inevitably be more plans than results.

Planning Ahead

A second group of activities could not show results as quickly because they needed thorough organizing in advance. Two quite different examples illustrate this, the travelling cinema and the organization of a county sports day, both of which were intended to take place in the summer of 1920. Like the examples described above, they represent different types of participation, but both seem to have been very effective ways of 'creating enthusiasm' (in the words of Burdon-Evans). This was both an end in itself and a necessary means of getting people involved in other activities. Most sporting fixtures fell into this category too, although not necessarily intentionally. A serious attempt was made immediately to co-opt and adapt existing football arrangements into leagues run by the County Association but in most sports more persuasion or work in establishing affiliated groups was needed to provide a foundation for competitions.

Cinema

The travelling cinema hit the road in the spring of 1920. Films were obtained free of charge from Famous Players

Productions Ltd, Cardiff, and they were shown in whatever premises could be found. These included local village halls, where they existed, and a drill hall in Llanfyllin. Even outdoor showings were contemplated, in Montgomery and Llanidloes. Buying, adapting and equipping a lorry for the purpose cost almost £1,490, equivalent to approximately £65,000 in 2018, and it needed a team of two people to operate it.[7] The programme began in Caersws in April 1920, moving on to another eleven locations that month, all for two nights each. It continued in this vein until June, visiting twenty-seven locations in all. Most of them booked repeat visits, and one was a special showing for David Davies's re-union with the men of his battalion. Forden was one of those places that booked return visits. On the second visit to the village, the press reported enthusiastic response to a very varied programme at the congregational hall that included Fatty Arbuckle in 'His Wedding Night' and 'Good Night Nurse'; a thriller featuring Dorothy Dalton, 'The Kaiser's Shadow'; Uncle Tom's Cabin; and a travel piece described as 'Hunting Kangaroos from Motor Cars'.

The Montgomeryshire travelling cinema programme was interrupted in late summer (August to October) by a three-month 'Roving Trip' out of the county to north and north-west Wales. This attracted great interest, encouraging attendance – especially in the seaside towns of Towyn and Porthmadog, although less so in smaller locations such as Beddgelert – and a cash surplus. It may be because of this demand for stimulating entertainment that, in autumn 1920, Major Davies presented a lorry to be set up as a second travelling cinema, to be fitted out for another 'Roving Trip'. It was enthusiastically received.[8] Meanwhile, the Montgomeryshire programme resumed for a winter season running from November 1920 to February 1921. The Christmas Day show in Llanfair was especially popular, generating the highest receipts of the season. By January, enthusiasm was still running high: there was standing room only at the first showing in Castle Caereinion, where more than 200 people crowded into the schoolroom to watch 'The Eternal City' and 'Vesuvius in Eruption'.[9] Responses such as these meant the eleven-month programme was judged a great success. At the same time, it suggested that with more suitable premises to accommodate similar entertainments, large numbers could be persuaded to participate in recreational events.

Sports Clubs and Leagues

A key object of the County Association was to establish leagues and competitions in a range of winter and summer sports. Attacking this task began almost immediately, getting together an array of committees (made up of volunteers and many club representatives) to do so. To make a quick start they co-opted existing arrangements in one way or another. The 'Football Sub-committee' itself was an example of this, being made up of club representatives already serving on existing football bodies in the county – the Montgomeryshire and District League and the Montgomeryshire Challenge Cup. However, the Association also tried supplementing existing arrangements. For example, in football it planned a Junior League, and supplemented that with a new Senior League for the benefit of a few clubs – Llanfyllin, Pant, Welshpool and Montgomery – which couldn't afford the existing arrangements. The aim was in part to prevent the new Junior league from being overwhelmed by Senior players with no league club to play for, a practice that generated a great deal of controversy in the local press and which the MCRA viewed as disruptive to the Juniors. By December 1919, they had planned not just football fixtures, but also a ladies' hockey knock-out competition, with seven teams having entered (Newtown, Montgomery and the County Schools of Newtown, Welshpool, Machynlleth, Chirbury and Caersws). At the same time, a Summer Sports Committee focused on setting up cricket leagues, a tennis county championship structure, and a County Quoiting Championship, while considering the equally important issue of which county gentlemen would present trophies.

Persuading the clubs to enter was another job entirely. By mid-March 1920, only Newtown and Llandinam Cricket Clubs had decided to join the new league, but with some encouragement five more were recruited by the end of the month (Caersws, Abermule, Chirbury,

Llanfyllin and Forden). In the end, the planned timetable was too ambitious, and formation of both senior and junior cricket leagues had to be postponed until a future year.[10] A knock-out competition was held instead. Later in 1920 the football clubs came fully on board, with both the Montgomeryshire and District League and the Montgomeryshire Challenge Cup affiliating. In November 1920, the minutes report more success with junior football, having restarted the Junior League. This extended its coverage as far as Aberystwyth and Towyn in a new 'Coast District', and a new league for village clubs was set up. These were the established sports of the county, generating almost as many column inches in the local press then as now. The offside rule and the merits of individual players were debated enthusiastically in post-war coverage.

While all were keen to resume sporting events that had been on hold since the outbreak of war in 1914, the County Association had to work hard to offer to these sports improvements or new developments that justified what might have been perceived as unwarranted intrusion. The exhibition match in September 1920 was one such offering, bringing a leading team to Newtown and creating an opportunity to create a county team. About 2,000 spectators were attracted to the match between West Bromwich Albion (Reserves) and Montgomery County. The visitors won 3-1, without any difficulty if the *County Times* correspondent is to be believed. All agreed that the match was an excellent means of stimulating local sport, as well as making a good day out.[11]

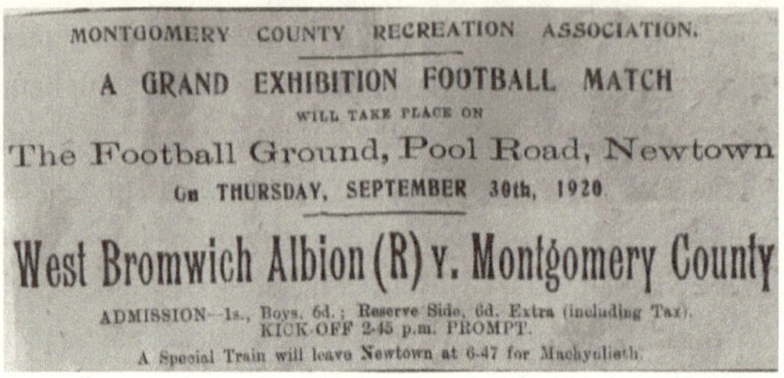

MONTGOMERY COUNTY RECREATION ASSOCIATION.

A GRAND EXHIBITION FOOTBALL MATCH

WILL TAKE PLACE ON

The Football Ground, Pool Road, Newtown

On THURSDAY, SEPTEMBER 30th, 1920.

West Bromwich Albion (R) v. Montgomery County

ADMISSION—1s., Boys, 6d.; Reserve Side, 6d. Extra (including Tax).
KICK-OFF 2-45 p.m. PROMPT.

A Special Train will leave Newtown at 6-47 for Machynlleth.

Grand Exhibition Football Match (*County Times,* 25 September 1920)

Another initiative entailed dealing with transport difficulties for teams and their supporters in a rural county with a dispersed population. Even where the locations were connected by railway, services did not run at suitable times for fixtures and not all clubs could afford it anyway. One of these problems the County Association could and did address directly by arranging with Cambrian Railways for special trains, such as later Saturday services. This was the kind of co-ordination that allowed the MCRA to make a case for its involvement in recreational activities, but it was a type of intervention that benefited other activities too, such as the organization of a New Year's Day train for the 1920 Newtown Eisteddfod committee.[12]

Sports with less established county structures, such as tennis and quoits, were easier to arrange. The most enthusiastic start was in quoits, where fifteen clubs entered the County Championship, which was a new venture for the county, forming a new quoits association to do so. Not all calls for new sporting ventures were taken up, however. Boxing is a notable omission from the programme of sports; there had been calls for a boxing structure and facilities to be set up since the inaugural meeting, but there is no evidence that it was ever promoted by the County Association, whereas the newly-formed motor cycling and air rifle clubs received an enthusiastic welcome.

The re-structuring of sporting activity continued in the Association's second year. For instance, growing interest in hockey meant that two leagues could be run instead of one. In senior football, the Association fell in line with the plans of the Football Association of Wales and changed the structure of their league from a County League to a two-part league that encompassed teams in western counties, from Aberystwyth to Towyn and even Porthmadoc.[13] Captain Jones reported in 1921 that football was now a 'large machine' that took up a lot of his time, noting that it was too early to judge its financial success, but the effort was justified by its popularity.[14]

County Sports Day

The establishment of leagues turned out to entail longer-term plans than initially envisaged, but there was no such problem with the MCRA's first County Sports

Day. This had a much clearer timetable, being scheduled for 17 July 1920, and it was an event that involved an enormous amount of participation in its planning, let alone on the day itself. A good ground was available for the event. The Royal Welsh Warehouse Recreation Society had decided not to revive its successful Annual Sports and Music Festival, which had run for many years before the war, and instead loaned its ground and equipment to the MCRA for the occasion.

By April 1920, the Summer Sports committee had recruited many people to its ranks in the interests of organizing the sports day. This involved organizing ground management, schedules, refreshments, prizes and finances (each overseen by a sub-committee of volunteers). Many participated on the day in roles such as stewards and time-keepers. The events and contests would broadly consist of a range of athletics, cycling, tug-of-war and brass band contests. In the interests of promoting the long-term standing of the event, athletics contests and prizes were conducted under the rules of the national athletics associations to which they affiliated.[15] There would also be entertainments: Newtown Silver Band was engaged for a half day, there would be alcoholic drinks and other refreshments

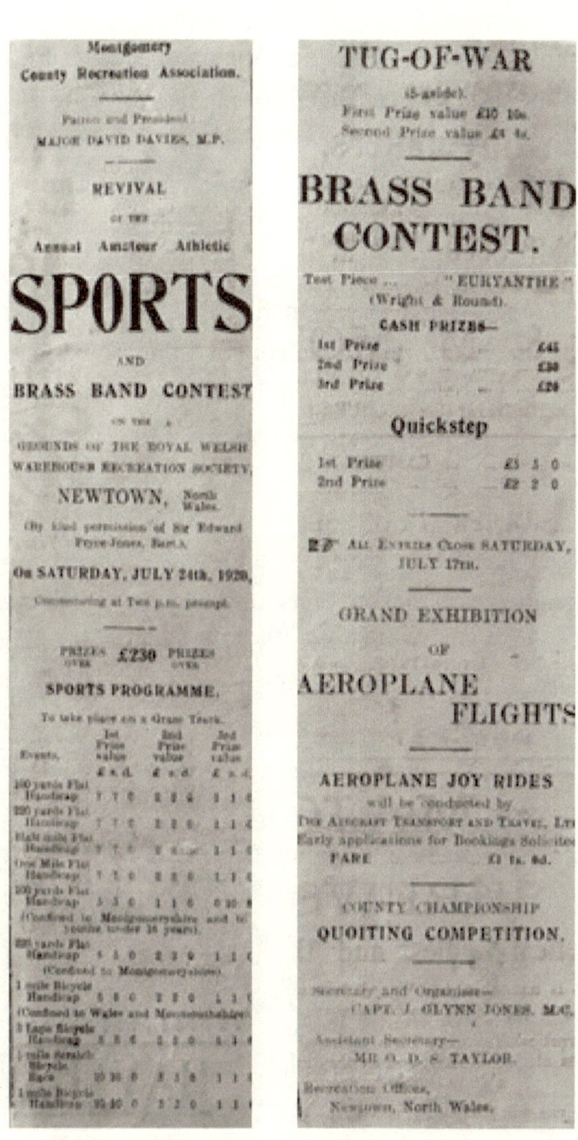

Montgomery
County Recreation Association.

Patron and President:
MAJOR DAVID DAVIES, M.P.

REVIVAL
OF THE
Annual Amateur Athletic

SPORTS

AND

BRASS BAND CONTEST

ON THE
GROUNDS OF THE ROYAL WELSH
WAREHOUSE RECREATION SOCIETY,

NEWTOWN, North Wales.

(By kind permission of Sir Edward Pryce-Jones, Bart.),

On SATURDAY, JULY 24th, 1920,

Commencing at Two p.m. prompt.

PRIZES OVER £230 PRIZES OVER

SPORTS PROGRAMME.

To take place on a Grass Track.

TUG-OF-WAR
(8-aside).
First Prize value £10 10s.
Second Prize value £4 4s.

BRASS BAND
CONTEST.

Test Piece ... "EURYANTHE"
(Wright & Round).

CASH PRIZES—

1st Prize	£45
2nd Prize	£30
3rd Prize	£20

Quickstep

1st Prize	£5 5 0
2nd Prize	£2 2 0

All Entries Close SATURDAY, JULY 17th.

GRAND EXHIBITION
OF
AEROPLANE
FLIGHTS

AEROPLANE JOY RIDES
will be conducted by
The Aircraft Transport and Travel, Ltd.
Early applications for Bookings Solicited.
FARE £1 1s. 0d.

COUNTY CHAMPIONSHIP
QUOITING COMPETITION.

Secretary and Organiser—
CAPT. J. GLYNN JONES, M.C.

Assistant Secretary—
MR. O. D. S. TAYLOR.

Recreation Offices,
Newtown, North Wales.

County Sports Day (*Montgomeryshire Express,* 13 July 1920)

available, as well as evening dancing. The star turn was to be an aeroplane, engaged to conduct 'Joy Rides', to be priced at one guinea for five minutes, and twice that sum for twenty minutes. Aeroplane displays were very popular attractions and could be relied on to draw a crowd, so this was important for reviving the festival as a self-supporting event.[16] In the event, it was a great disappointment to the organizers and the crowd that the aeroplane did not turn up, the press worrying that the failure of the main attraction might reduce attendance the following year.

Press coverage suggests that organizing the event was challenging for the secretary and his newly-appointed assistant.[17] The Royal Welsh Warehouse Recreation Society had run the pre-war festival so successfully that they had a wealth of experience, with their key people described in the press as almost 'permanent officials'; it is not clear from the records whether any of them were involved in the MCRA, but the implication of press reports is that despite being a revival of the fixture, it was in many ways a new undertaking with new men (and few women).[18] The same applied to the competitions themselves: the *County Times* correspondent mourned the loss of the familiar competitors of the past, but after six years had passed the competitions were dominated, unsurprisingly, by a new generation.[19]

Changed economic conditions also had an impact, especially on the willingness of bands to travel from the colliery districts in south Wales. There was considerable anxiety about this among the organizers. In May 1920, one of their number, Harry Morris, was despatched to Mountain Ash 'to attend the Brass Band contest on Whit Monday, with a view to inducing the bands to enter' the MCRA competition.[20] His encouragement was not enough on its own: the secretary had to offer additional prizes to attract Welsh band entrants, as by 13 July it was still unclear whether there would be entrants from Wales at all, the main problem being expense. This succeeded in getting entries from the Parc & Dare and the Ynyshir Standard Colliery bands in the Rhondda, but others decided they could not afford the trip. A second consideration may have been the absence of cheap excursion trains, which railway companies had offered before the war.[21] Nonetheless, with two English bands as well (Wingates from Lancashire and Fodens Motor Works of Northwich), the competition could at least go ahead.

The County Sports Day turned out to be a success. The *Express* gave it a glowing report, while the *County Times* was more measured in its congratulations. It was held on a rare dry and sunny day in an otherwise miserably wet summer, and approximately 7,500-8,000 people attended, despite the lack of cheap transport and choral concerts. In spite of these setbacks, there was a small surplus of £29, which was considered satisfactory, and a result that could be improved upon in future years.[22] Its success was followed the next year by the news that David Davies had persuaded the Royal Welsh Warehouse to part with the ground. He purchased it and presented it to the MCRA as the new County Ground on condition it was always used for 'recreative' purposes.[23] The future seemed secure.

Aftermath

Despite an encouraging start, the intention that the County Sports Day should be the foundation of an enduring annual and self-sustaining event came to nothing. After making arrangements for the 1921 event, this time to include choral concerts as well, it was decided the following June to abandon it, having already postponed it to August, owing to strikes in the coal industry and concerns about growing unemployment in the county. The strikes meant, among other things, the absence of colliery and industrial brass bands, and possibly no trains as so many had been cancelled owing to lack of coal. Fewer people had the means to attend anyway, locally or from further afield, and perhaps there was less appetite to do so. Another attempt was made to revive it the following year, but this time it was hit by very wet weather. Attendance was much lower, around 5,000 in all, and excursions from Birmingham and south Wales attracted only three hundred of those. As a result, it is likely that it struggled financially. David Davies used the 1922 event to again publicize the gift of the

County Ground, when he ceremonially handed over the deeds to the Association's trustees.[24] David Pugh suggests that a Sports Day ran until 1925, with diminished attendance, but those events do not appear in the Association's remaining minutes or accounts, and their status is unclear.[25] It is clear, however, that after the cancellation of the 1921 event, the County Sports Day did not regain its former prestige, and could not be sustained as the flagship annual event that the Association had envisaged.

The cinema project suffered a similar fate. It had been successful enough to justify planning a repeat of both the county and roving tours in 1921-2, yet it did not run again. The MCRA's annual report for 1922 notes that operations were suspended while searching for a lighter set of equipment, the original plant having been found to be too heavy and expensive to run.[26] None was ever obtained, and two years later the existing equipment was sold at a considerable loss.[27] The records are silent on the reasons for halting the programme, although it is clear from the accounts that it was not a profitable enterprise. Running costs were high and expensive repairs were needed, especially before the plant was sold, so it may have been badly damaged. The intention had been that the cinema would become financially viable, and apart from the donation of a lorry, it was funded by means of a loan. With variable demand for the travelling cinema in the county and a worsening local economy in the early 1920s, the delay in searching for better equipment may simply have been long enough for the MCRA to conclude that it could not be financially viable until conditions improved.

Although these eye-catching and entertaining activities did not continue, they proved successful in generating enthusiasm and community involvement. They were equally successful in keeping the County Association in the public eye and generating positive coverage in the columns of the local newspapers. However, they also illustrate a potential tension between the level of financial support the entire scheme required and the income the constituent activities could generate directly. Even in the case of the very popular football leagues, it was still not clear in 1921 whether they would be financially viable. In the meantime, the foundations of a county-wide network of local recreation associations were being laid, and the Association had made progress with its longer-term plans to develop infrastructure. These would mean that eventually some activities could be organized in the localities where they took place, while others were replaced by new initiatives.

The Railway Network

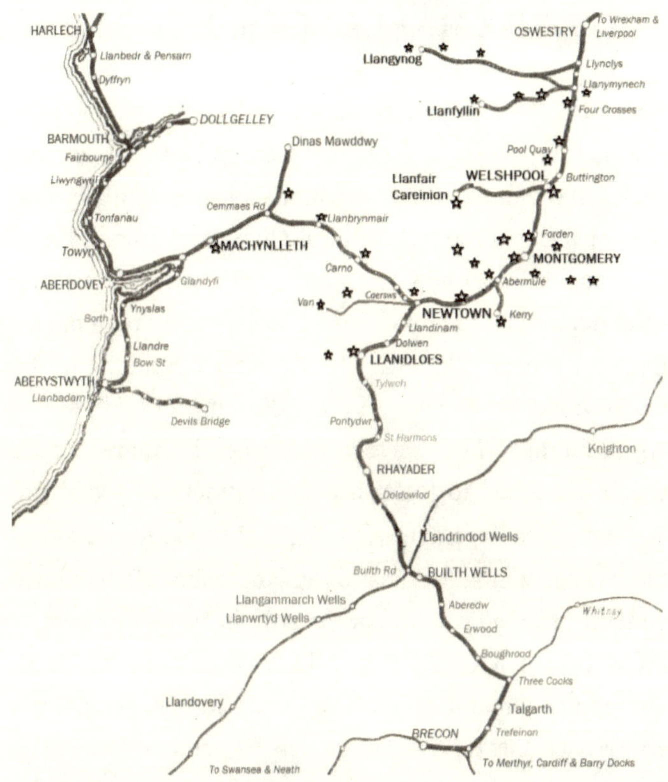

Montgomeryshire in the 1920s was well connected by railway to all parts of Wales, to Liverpool and Cheshire via Oswestry, and Birmingham via Shrewsbury. Some connecting lines are omitted from this map of the Cambrian Railways network, especially those linking with Shrewsbury, but the connectedness of the key towns in the county is nonetheless clear. Each asterisk indicates the location of a Recreation Association that was affiliated to the MCRA in the 1920s.

Map adapted from C. P. Gasquoine, *The Story of The Cambrian*, 1922, Project Gutenberg eText 20074.

3: EXPANSION, ACHIEVEMENTS AND CHALLENGES, 1920-22

Some calls for voluntary action following the 1914-18 war had their roots in ideas that were intended to achieve social and cultural transformation, but it is unlikely that the concerns of the Agricultural Club were among them. This august body was more concerned with combatting rural depopulation and its impact on agriculture, a matter that had concerned David Davies at the beginning of the century. At its meeting in London in July 1918, the Agricultural Club agreed that social centres were urgently needed to foster the development of social life and activities in rural areas.[1] This led to the formation of the Village Clubs Association in November 1919, whose general principles were comparable in many respects to those of the MCRA. David Davies was among those who read a paper at the new Village Clubs Association's conference the following year, in November 1920. The 'great and the good' dominated reports of the conference, their contributions ranging from nostalgia for 'Merrie England' that even the *County Times* found hard to take, to the pragmatic observation that unless rural life was made more tolerable, they would not get 'the new class of intelligent labourer' that was needed.[2] Davies focused on the particular need for village halls and playing fields, and the advantages of creating a federation of county associations. By then the MCRA, with Davies's backing, had already made progress in each of these areas.

Local Associations

Having started with the county association, in practice 'federation' in Montgomeryshire meant establishing a network of local associations. These were the necessary prerequisites for self-sustaining locally-run village institutes and playing fields. In this respect, the MCRA had similar principles to the Village Clubs Association: the club or association should be self-supporting and run by a committee of members from the locality. It is not clear whether the MCRA adopted the full set of principles espoused by the Village Clubs Association, which held that institutes should be free from elements of patronage and that all inhabitants of the village 'without distinction of class or opinion, and when practicable of both sexes' should be eligible for membership. But the reports and correspondence of successive MCRA secretaries suggest the same ideas were applied.[3]

The foundations of a county-wide network of local recreation associations were laid while plans for sports, lectures and cinema were being put into action and enthusiastically reported. Captain Jones reported having spent most of his time in the first five months of the MCRA in forming these local associations.[4] The process began with holding public meetings to explain the scheme and drum up support, followed by visiting each locality where an interest had been expressed in forming a local association. His itinerary indicates that he visited most villages in the county to explain the objects of the association,[5] and he continued to hold regular meetings with the resulting associations. It was a top-down exercise. The MCRA decided which applicants it considered suitable to become local associations – that is, which ones were plausibly self-supporting. For instance, a group at Marton-in-the Chirbury wanted to affiliate, but it was considered too small and was told to amalgamate with the Chirbury association. Local associations would not be centrally subsidized, and so they would need to raise funds for their activities themselves, through donations, sponsorship and fundraising events. They were envisaged as co-ordinating groups within each locality, the idea being not just to bring together existing interests but to develop new activities as well. Consequently, they needed a strong base of energetic members. They were also envisaged as part of an emphatically hierarchical structure, set out in a detailed pamphlet produced by Captain Glynn Jones.[6]

These efforts were repaid by growing interest. The MCRA's first annual general meeting in 1920 reported that twenty-seven local associations had formed and affiliated to the county association,[7] which in turn affiliated on their behalf to the Village Clubs Association.[8] The connection with that association was cultivated for a while; the secretary reported visiting their distinguished president and secretary (Sir Henry Rew and the Hon. R. E. S. Barrington, DSO, respectively) and reported that they were keen to 'get all Welsh Counties in line with ours', and had recently appointed a Welsh organizer to that end.[9] Apart from building its profile in London decision-making circles, cultivating this link meant that the MCRA would also benefit from the Village Clubs Association's advice and its ability to obtain advantageous terms on essential recreational supplies for the local associations.[10] By the time David Davies addressed the Village Clubs conference, the number of local associations affiliated to the MCRA had reached forty-one,[11] after which growth slowed. By the following spring the number had risen to forty-two.[12]

The raised profile of these activities also meant that there were applications to affiliate from outside the county, from Bishops Castle (in Shropshire) and Dinas Mawddwy (in Merionethshire). Both were turned down, with varying degrees of regret, on the grounds that it would be misusing David Davies' generosity. Federation was not entirely trouble-free. Captain Jones related concerns about the relative weakness of some local branches, about many being focused entirely on sporting activity rather than including intellectual recreation, and about the frequent attempts to introduce sectarian, political or class divisions, all of which could be overcome with persistence.[13] The top-down approach adopted by Captain Jones, which perhaps reflected his formative military experience, may itself have contributed to these difficulties. While it was effective in the short run, by the time of the second annual meeting Burdon-Evans thought that an autocratic approach was no longer necessary and argued for a more democratic organization.[14] Nonetheless, a functioning recreational structure had been put together in the MCRA's first year and it benefited from widespread support and sympathetic reporting in the local and national press.

Grounds

Recreation grounds, or playing fields, were essential to the physical recreation objectives the MCRA intended local associations to carry out. One of the principles set out in the guide for local associations was that grounds should, wherever possible, be owned, and certainly managed, by the local association. Where the MCRA owned the grounds, management should be with the local groups, although in practice occasionally disputes arose about ground management. Some of the work undertaken by local associations to develop land that had been donated into recreation grounds was funded by loans from the MCRA. For example, Machynlleth recreation ground was laid out in 1920 with loans of £150 from the MCRA. Another £50 was advanced for a tennis pavilion, although it is not clear how that affected the cricket club from whom they bought the pavilion.

The grounds in MCRA ownership were either donated directly or bought with funds donated for that purpose. The earliest of these were acquired in December 1919 when David Davies presented the MCRA with grounds at Caersws, Machynlleth and Llandinam, his estate employees doing some of the work needed on the cricket pitch at the latter. In 1920, a field at Berriew was purchased by the MCRA for £200, to be leased to the local association.[15] Other areas of the county also badly needed grounds. The secretary drew particular attention to Chirbury and Montgomery, where suitable land was in the estate of the Earls of Powys. Nor was the need for grounds confined to the villages alone. Grounds in Welshpool were acquired from the Earls of Powys with the aid of a donation from David Davies in 1922.[16] The presentation by David Davies of the county ground in 1921, detailed in chapter 2, was gratefully received. So too was a parcel of land that would become the Newtown Football Ground, purchased from 'four gentlemen' who had bought it to reserve it for the MCRA, and handed it over for 'practically a nominal sum'.[17] This relatively short list of grounds in the hands of the MCRA is no indicator of the overall picture. Land donated to local associations directly is rarely recorded in MCRA archives, so the full extent of support for the recreation movement or network in the county cannot be assessed here.

Village Institutes

Among the motivations for so many localities to affiliate to the MCRA in its first year was the prospect of being eligible for subsidized new village institutes, to be erected by the MCRA. The expectation that David Davies would provide the subsidy was widely reported. The institute was to be a non-denominational village facility. At a minimum, there should be some kind of hall, ideally with more than one room to allow multiple activities, such as billiards, drama and choir rehearsals, educational use and perhaps a small library, as well as a basic kitchen. Ideally, these should be permanent, solid structures.

A small sub-committee explored the possibilities for erecting permanent and temporary institutes early in 1920, concluding that given the cost of building and the number of locations in need of an institute (as well as other unspecified difficulties), temporary wooden buildings might be advisable. It was thought important to capitalize on the early enthusiasm rather than wait until sufficient funds for permanent buildings could be raised; in this way the temporary building could become the venue for fundraising events for its permanent replacement. Burdon-Evans proposed buying surplus army huts, which were now available in large numbers and within reasonable distance since the end of the war. This suggestion received cautious agreement from the sub-committee.

Perhaps those without military experience did not share the major's confidence in the suitability of army huts, and they thought it wise to consult the building foreman at the Llandinam Estate, Mr Parfitt, before going ahead with the purchase of one army hut on an experimental basis.[18] The secretary also consulted the Welsh Housing Trust in Cardiff, where he was able to look at plans and obtain advice on the work necessary to convert army huts into village institutes.

The first experimental institute building was offered to Abermule, where it was duly erected and was the first to open on 11 November 1920. The sub-committee was already sufficiently convinced by the experiment to be able to confirm in July 1920 the purchase and allocation of eight army huts of varying descriptions and sizes to priority localities. By then the secretary reported that he had visited nearly every village in the county, and that the huts were in the process of being erected at Caersws and Van, as well as at Abermule. Different arrangements were made for Tregynon, where stables on the Gregynog estate were to be converted into an institute, with an extension constructed from one half-sized hut. The sub-committee also agreed to purchase a further eleven huts for nominated associations, and to reserve eight more should the associations in question be able to secure suitable sites, noting the sizes and associations for which they were earmarked.[19]

At that stage, there were potentially twenty-five new temporary institutes in the pipeline, including those already started, some to be constructed from more than one hut. In another twenty-nine localities it was decided that a new institute was not yet needed, although one of these (Arddleen) did soon succeed in acquiring one – it was opened in October 1921. At the same time, model trust deeds were drawn up and furniture and equipment was sourced. This included billiard tables for some locations and a very large quantity of army chairs and benches everywhere. The workload these numbers imply – at the same time as organizing the Sports Day and other schemes – most likely contributed to the Association's decision to appoint an assistant secretary in March 1920. It is not clear from the remaining records how many village huts were in fact erected; the latest minutes to recount progress on the Institutes scheme refer to twenty-two in total, but only seventeen of those can be identified with certainty.[20]

The institutes made an immediate impact. On the opening of the first institute, the *County Times* remarked that 'Armistice Day marked an epoch in the village life of Abermule, as on that day there was formally opened in that village a memorial hall'.[21] The characteristically more effusive *Express* declared that '[u]pon Abermule falls the honour of being the first village to possess a hut ready for occupation, and it was a joyful day for the inhabitants', despite the tears shed at the unveiling of the war memorial tablet. It was reported that the MCRA defrayed half the cost, and the land was made available at a nominal cost by the county authority. The Caersws institute opened a few weeks later, in early December 1920. The *Express* reported that in this instance the site was given by Edward Jones of Maesmawr, one of the MCRA's trustees. The institute was much admired, as it could 'scarcely be recognised' as a former army hut 'by reason of its resplendence in fresh paint'. Having three rooms – a billiard room, scouts room/gymnasium, kitchen – and electric light, it was a big improvement on the existing village hall, which was not big enough for billiards. There were speeches, everyone was praised, and it seems all had a good time.

David Davies' speech explained that owing to the high cost of building it was impossible to erect village halls of a permanent character, and he expressed his hope that the new institute 'would serve for a considerable number of years ... they were a start'. He was 'sure that permanent structures would follow in their train'.[22] Reports on the Llanbrynmair opening on Christmas Day echoed those constraints, saying 'there is nothing like a stone building, which had been the dream of twenty years ago', but this was 'the only building possible in these days'. That regret did not prevent Llanbrynmair from holding a party – the institute was not quite complete, but it had a platform big enough for a choir and was packed to its 600-person capacity.[23]

An opening with a slightly different atmosphere took place at the smaller New Mills institute on Boxing Day 1920, which the local association asked Captain Jones to open. As the *Express* reported, his speech turned out to be a rousing tribute to youth:

> *It was just three months back since he had visited New Mills through the mist and rain, to meet half-a-dozen young fellows who said they were anxious to have an institute. His advice at the time was that if they did, then they must go for it like a bull at a haystack, and not listen to the carping of a few grumblers ... he had no hesitation in describing them as young men with a vision.*

The guests remarked on the standard of the building, which according to the *Express* seemed to be a labour of love as well as of sinews. The chairman of the association, Mr E. Evans of Temperance House, was astonished by the 'remarkable transformation of the army hut first viewed on the grey common at Prees Heath into the cosy institute set in its present prim and picturesque situation'. The opening was quite a party, with the novelty of (temporary) electric lighting for the day, and it included a tea and an evening eisteddfod. The hall would hold 300 people. Nonetheless, Captain Jones hoped they would now press on to raise the funds for a permanent institute, this building being only a temporary one. In an interesting coda, perhaps suggesting where the motivation for such hard work came from, the Captain commented that apart from MCRA business meetings, this was the first public gathering he had been to since he returned from the front.[24]

Press reports highlight the range of people who came together to create these facilities. Other sources draw attention to the various ways in which young people were central to the ambitions of the entire venture. The *Express* reported Capt. Jones saying, in the course of a discussion relating to representation on committees, that '[w]hen one considers things … it will be found that ex-service men are the most prominent figures in the acquiring of institutes. The young people do the work.'[25] This, and the New Mills institute, certainly reflected his own priorities for the MCRA, which were bound up with opportunities for young people of all ages. In his reports he deplored scenes of roaming children and of young boys hanging about corners of village streets making it 'most objectionable for young girls to pass', but he was clear in blaming this on a lack of facilities and managed activities. Institutes were part of the answer to this perceived problem. They would be the sites of all manner of organized sports and activity that should have a profound educational and moral impact.

In practice, both Capt. Jones and David Davies were keen to see the MCRA promote the Boy Scout movement, and to a lesser extent the Girl Guides, and were equally keen that the MCRA should visibly align itself with the movement. This policy began early. The organizer for Wales of the Boy Scouts Association, Mr E. Samuels, was invited to speak at the first annual meeting in 1920,[26] sparking a slew of letters and articles in the local press defending the movement against those who perceived it as militaristic. Although the Scout movement was independent, Davies (who was District Commissioner for the Boy Scouts) promised to donate £50 to the Association for promoting the Boy Scout movement in connection with the MCRA. At that stage the only Boy Scout troop in the county was the one run by Captain Jones at Caersws.[27]

Funding Institutes

Press reports on the new institutes also illuminate the extent to which the entire project depended on localities being able to get hold of a site for little or no financial outlay; donations such as the land at Guilsfield presented by Colonel Mytton were gratefully received.[28] There are hints that the MCRA committee members drew on their social contacts, and those of their president and trustees, to encourage such donations. That is the most that can be gleaned from the MCRA records, since the sites were generally conveyed directly to the local association, whether they were donated or sold to them.

Institutes were provided on the basis that the MCRA would cover half of the total cost of erecting them. Local associations would meet the other half of the cost, but at the outset would only have to find half of that (a quarter of the total cost); the MCRA would make a loan for the remaining quarter of the cost, which the local association was to repay at an agreed rate.[29] There were some planned exceptions – at Carno and Montgomery, where David Davies had made promises before the war that the MCRA would fulfill by paying in full for the institutes. Financial records survive for just a few of the early institutes: Abermule cost £732 in total, Caersws £832 in the same year, while the more unusual Tregynon conversion and extension project came to over £1,500. The army huts themselves accounted for only a small fraction of the cost. For instance, at Caersws the huts cost £91, while the rest of the expenditure went on labour, transport, fees and additional materials. At Abermule more expensive huts were used but lower carriage and materials costs were incurred.

By 1925, the MCRA had incurred over £23,500 of expenditure on institutes, excluding any amounts that may have been charged to the accounts before 1921.[30] This amount is consistent with the construction of the eighteen to twenty-two institutes referred to earlier. It was a large investment: equivalent to well over £1 million in 2019 terms.[31]

Comparable amounts of special donations were recorded in the period 1919-21.[32] These are consistent with Captain Jones's assurance in July 1920 that the MCRA had 'every reason to believe that the expenses incurred in the provision of these institutes will not come out of the ordinary funds of the Association'.[33] That would prove essential, since the rising costs of materials and labour through 1920 and 1921 meant they cost far more than initially expected. The implication of press coverage is that the special funds would be donated by David Davies. An alternative suggestion is made by H. Noel Jerman in an earlier history of the MCRA, in which he claimed that the MCRA received assistance on a pound for pound basis from the Development Commission.

The Development Commission was set up by the government in 1909 to assist viable schemes to improve rural life.[34] There is an ambiguous reference to this source of funding in the surviving MCRA minutes, and the earliest accounting records are too fragmentary to definitively attribute all sources of income. However, press reports detail an 'arrangement' put together by Burdon-Evans and Sir Henry Rew, chairman of the Village Clubs Association, to enable the latter to obtain match funding on a pound-for-pound basis from the Development Commission. The essence of this arrangement was that the MCRA would make a sizeable donation to the Village Clubs Association, which would later return the donation, and the two associations would split the Development Commission grant between them.[35] The outcome of this plan is not known. It is unlikely that the MCRA obtained a significant sum from this source, but it is plausible that the source accounts for some or all of the £1,900 of unattributed donations in 1921-22. The remainder of the MCRA's funding came from members of the Davies family, amounting to over £11,000 in that year alone.[36]

Although the Village Clubs Association had obtained a grant from the Development Commission to assist with setting up, it certainly experienced considerable difficulty in extracting funds thereafter, obtaining just £20,611 between 1919 and 1924.[37] That made it difficult to fund the 300 or more village clubs affiliated to it. Writing in 1921, the Village Clubs' secretary, Harold Lacey, identified obtaining premises as a central problem for villages. The high cost of building was prohibitive, and 'although disused army huts are said to exist in thousands, the villages experience the greatest difficulty in obtaining them'.[38] It also turned out that the cost of army huts was high, in precisely the period and places they were most needed. But with the substantial funding provided by David Davies, there was less difficulty obtaining them in Montgomeryshire. They also turned out to be a more enduring contribution to the community than initially expected, as most of these 'temporary' buildings were still in use thirty years later, and a few lasted much longer.

Van Institute in 2019. The only MCRA institute building retaining the original structure or features at the MCRA's centenary, when it was still in use. (Courtesy of Dr John Hughes)

Music

Among the MCRA's early supporters were many who hoped to see more music-making in the county. The 'present conditions' of music in the county were reviewed as the starting point for a comprehensive scheme of work, and the results were not encouraging. There were, for instance, only three bands – a good silver band at Newtown and brass bands at Llanidloes and Machynlleth. Within six months, two new brass bands had been formed at Llandinam and Montgomery, and there were plans to set up another at Welshpool. These were the Association's first forays into supporting music-making, when David Davies presented two collections of four brass instruments, which were in turn presented to Llandinam and Machynlleth bands.[39] To further the cause, he also donated £50 to the Association for each affiliated band, which it loaned (rather than donated) to the new Montgomery and Welshpool bands.

Choral Societies seemed to be in better shape. The review identified seven (at Newtown, Caersws, Welshpool, Llandinam, Llanbrynmair, Four Crosses and Llanfair) but nonetheless it was thought that these were fewer than could be expected. Orchestral music was regarded as being in a dismal state: although there had been some before the war the reviewers concluded that '[i]nstrumental work in the County may be regarded as dead'.[40] More encouragingly, they found evidence that in some places there was a desire for tuition. They had also reviewed the school music curriculum at elementary and secondary levels, where they noted that although music was on the curriculum and part of the teachers' leaving certificate, what was taught was often quite limited. Compounding this, the education authorities had not appointed or even mooted travelling teachers of vocal or instrumental music. These shortcomings were more fundamental than a lack of instruments.

These problems, and more importantly ideas that would inform a scheme to improve matters, were discussed at an informal conference held at Newtown in January 1920. This set out some important principles, drawing on advice from Dr Walford Davies, then Professor of Music at the University College of Wales, Aberystwyth and Director of the Welsh National Council for Music. The two central recommendations incorporated into the final scheme were that the MCRA should appoint a first-rate Director of Music for the county, and that it should run a county music festival to energize the musical efforts of the whole county, along the lines of the long-standing festival held at Harlech. But it was also emphasized that a scheme to promote music should include practical suggestions for better organization of teaching at elementary and intermediate levels, including the need for a government full-time music teacher for each county in Wales, as there was in Scotland. They noted, in brisk terms, that this 'should be as easy as it is overdue'.[41] The resulting scheme of work was agreed just in time to be announced to general satisfaction at the first annual meeting of the Association in July 1920.[42] By then, the organization of eisteddfodau had been added to the initial ambitions, along with drama and pageantry, but neither of the last two received any discernible attention from the music committee that was responsible for them.

In October 1920, the Music Organizer, Mr Nicholas, took up his post, beginning by starting tutorial classes in Llanidloes, Machynlleth and Newtown. By November, there had been a satisfying increase in the number of active choirs, twenty-four of which affiliated to the MCRA, and a programme was drawn up for the first county Music Festival, to be held in May 1921.[43] The plan for the music festival was reported in both local papers on several occasions, where there was more coverage of disagreements than in the MCRA minutes.

For instance, when Mr Nicholas outlined the planned programme for May 1921 there was some concern that it might be too ambitious.[44] Later, the festival date was changed to 21 July, although the records are silent on when and why. Perhaps it was related to an exchange of views with the Llanfyllin Eisteddfod Committee, the threat of strikes, or the availability of a venue. The festival would be held in Newtown, in a location that had still not been found by the beginning of 1921, one that would need to accommodate a crowd of six thousand and a choir over one thousand strong. Evidently, the Association had rejected the secretary's idea that it could take place at the County Ground as an outdoor event. Finding a location proved to be a difficult task. Eventually the need became so urgent that the secretary purchased an aircraft hangar, had it hauled from Lincoln, then erected, repaired and improved, all just in time.

The Festival

Individual choirs were to be chosen on their merits to give solo performances in the afternoon, while the evening was to be devoted to a performance of the massed choirs of the county. Organizing the festival took the greater part of the committee's time and a great deal of guidance by Walford Davies. Nineteen choirs – a combined chorus of some 1,100 singers – took part in a programme whose main work was Mendelssohn's *Hymn of Praise*, conducted by Walford Davies and Mr

Nicholas, and featuring first-rate soloists. Most of the rehearsals in the preceding year were conducted separately. The co-ordination of their efforts was achieved mainly by the music organizer visiting their separate rehearsals, and by staging some district rehearsals that combined two to four choirs.[45] Some choirs found the set works very difficult.[46] Given the earlier comments on orchestral music in the county, it is no surprise that the festival recruited musicians from elsewhere to supplement the orchestra. Most of these were professionals, but the organizer was very encouraged that sixty-three members of the orchestra were amateur Montgomeryshire musicians. He argued that this approach had a much greater educational benefit than the easier option of engaging a more polished professional orchestra, such as the Hallé, giving as it did the pleasure of helping to create and maintain widespread interest among residents of the county in learning and perfecting musical skills.[47]

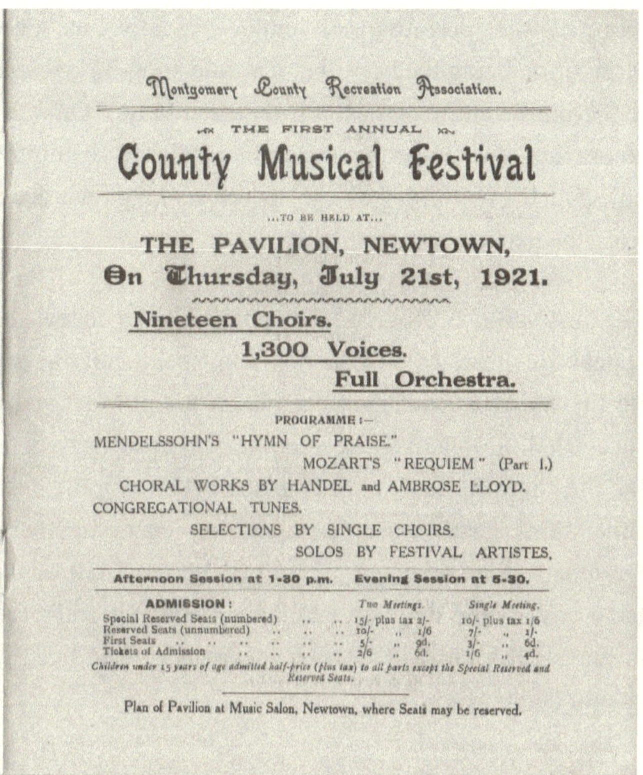

Montgomery County Recreation Association.

THE FIRST ANNUAL

County Musical Festival

...TO BE HELD AT...

THE PAVILION, NEWTOWN,
On Thursday, July 21st, 1921.

Nineteen Choirs.
1,300 Voices.
Full Orchestra.

PROGRAMME:—

MENDELSSOHN'S "HYMN OF PRAISE."
MOZART'S "REQUIEM" (Part I.)
CHORAL WORKS BY HANDEL and AMBROSE LLOYD.
CONGREGATIONAL TUNES.
SELECTIONS BY SINGLE CHOIRS.
SOLOS BY FESTIVAL ARTISTES.

Afternoon Session at 1-30 p.m. Evening Session at 5-30.

ADMISSION:	*Two Meetings.*	*Single Meeting.*
Special Reserved Seats (numbered)	15/- plus tax 2/-	10/- plus tax 1/6
Reserved Seats (unnumbered)	10/- „ 1/6	7/- „ 1/-
First Seats	5/- „ 9d.	3/- „ 6d.
Tickets of Admission	2/6 „ 6d.	1/6 „ 4d.

Children under 15 years of age admitted half-price (plus tax) to all parts except the Special Reserved and Reserved Seats.

Plan of Pavilion at Music Salon, Newtown, where Seats may be reserved.

The programme for the first County Music Festival

The period leading up to the festival was one of uncertainty because of the strikes taking place in coal-mining areas, but by 19 July the *Express* reported that with the strike over the Cambrian Railways was offering cheap rates for the festival period.[48] The festival itself was thought to have been a great success. The town and the Royal Welsh Warehouse were festooned with banners, and W. H. Leslie, president of the evening performance and the committee chairman, confessed himself 'a very unduly proud man'.[49] The *Express* reported the performances enthusiastically, its only reservation being the hope that it would soon be possible to recruit the entire orchestra from the county.[50] Only the comments of a Dolgellau correspondent, who seemingly objected to Walford Davies' speech-making, detracted from the general approval.[51]

The festival also provided an opportunity to renew the appeal for subscribers to the Pavilion, specifically to pay for the site. An appeal had been launched in May, and it succeeded in obtaining the support of Newtown traders. By the time the festival took place a list of more than fifty subscribers was displayed as encouragement. Eventually the Newtown subscribers raised £410 of the £550 cost of the Pavilion site, which was not conveyed to the MCRA until 1925, after the Pavilion had been in use for some years.[52]

The reporting and enthusiasm in 1921 were in the context of this being the first festival of its kind in the county. It was recognized, especially by the Music Organizer, that the performances were not perfect but that a very good start had been made. Enough had been achieved to persuade the performers and the audience to come back for more. Planning for the 1922 festival began in earnest in September 1921, focusing on selecting the programme, especially the main evening performance, and debating the inclusion of works that would be more accessible to village choirs. The date was moved to 17 May 1922, as so many members had found

July difficult because of the requirements of the agricultural year. This time they worked with the Powys Eisteddfod, which would be held on 1 June, to agree at least one piece of work in common, but there seems not to have been communication with the organizers of a children's choral festival in Llanidloes to be held on the same day, nor was the shorter rehearsal period available to choirs taken into account.

Unusually frank notes of a meeting reviewing the 1922 festival show a great deal of dissatisfaction among the choirs with the arrangement of the choral works and the late distribution of music. There was no criticism of the practical organization of the festival day, but distinct annoyance with a report by the organizer that criticized the choirs' performance in works they felt were badly arranged and poorly staged. It was in some ways a crisis meeting. Its background was a likely financial loss and lower ticket sales than in the previous year. Yet all agreed the festival should continue, and another emergency meeting on the subject took them to Gregynog to request more help from Walford Davies. The outcome was a list of proposals amounting to advice to hold their nerve. They selected Bach's *St Matthew's Passion* as the main work for 1923, and Mr Nicholas was demoted. The key achievement as far as the committee was concerned was that Walford Davies agreed to conduct the next festival and to assist with regional rehearsals.[53]

The gap between musical ambition and the inexperience of the choirs was still great, especially in the small village choirs. By February 1923, two choirs thought they would have to withdraw, as the difficulty of the work had caused members to leave, while several others found it very hard but were persevering for the time being. One conductor had been equally discouraged until he attended a conductors' conference that morning.[54] That final example illustrates the vital role of Walford Davies, who led that conference, in keeping up the morale of the dispersed choirs. It was effective but needed constant reinforcement through visits from the chairman and Mr Nicholas, and stirring letters from Sir Walford.[55] If there was any discontent after the 1923 festival, it was not reflected in the minute books. Mr Nicholas took the view that the worst was over, and the focus moved on to the next festival, to co-operation with the Powys Eisteddfod in selecting programmes, and with the new Cardiganshire festival in sharing the cost of soloists and orchestra. Interspersed among these decisions were attempts to raise more donations and sell more tickets, so that the festival could become profitable enough to be self-sustaining. Few of these initiatives succeeded in that aim.

The relationship of the festival to the MCRA was sometimes ambiguous. The MCRA had established a number of committees dealing with music in its central structure, yet the discussion in meetings that were largely composed of choir representatives was somewhat distanced from the central organization. The MCRA was seen as playing the role of financial guardian. The reporting structure suggests that the festival was intended to be a profit-making subsidiary operation along the same lines as the cinema, that is being a self-contained activity but not entirely independent. The Music Organizer was employed by the MCRA in the service of the music scheme as a whole, including its ambitions for education. In practice, the festival absorbed most of the time available to both committees and the organizer, and other aspects of the music programme did not progress as much as intended.

There were successes in starting music classes for young people in Newtown, Machynlleth and Llanidloes, in addition to the initial tutorial classes. A tutor was found to give violin classes in several locations. But the aim of intervening in or provoking improvement of school music education, on which everything else depended in the long run, moved more slowly. Captain Jones led a deputation to the local education authority in February 1921,[56] but although they succeeded in obtaining support in principle, it was not followed up with more definite plans. A report in December 1923 suggested where the education authority's efforts should be focused and it identified some scope for intervention by the music committee, but by then the festival was the MCRA's main contribution to musical education.

Infrastructure and Economic Context

The *Express* drew great meaning from the first festival. The accomplishments of the MCRA so far represented 'only the foundational work upon which a magnificent superstructure is being erected', it claimed, and the festival and Pavilion were 'an impressive stage of the process' of achieving this. That visionary interpretation of the early activities of the MCRA undervalues the enormous achievement represented by constructing a county-wide cultural and community infrastructure on a scale not previously attempted. It was achieved in challenging economic conditions that over the course of just a few years moved from the inflationary effect of materials and labour shortages of the immediate post-war years, to deflation, widespread strikes and the rapid decline of local industry. For instance, in the Llanidloes area alone, by 1921 factories were closing, much else was at a standstill, and with the mines at Van already closed, unemployment was rising rapidly. Agriculture was no safe haven either, as demonstrated by the falling value of land at this time.

The state of the economy goes a long way towards explaining why MCRA reports so often expressed disappointment in the financial support the organization received from the county. For instance, a letter to the Express by 'a local Secretary' was distressed by the 'wretched, discreditable' level of support shown for the MCRA in that year, when donations of £68 from the county were dwarfed by the sum of over £1,200 from Plas Dinam[57]. The support received from other sources was mainly directed to the local associations – rather than to the county association – in the form of land. Other correspondents located criticism of the MCRA in political opposition to David Davies[58]. The MCRA began as a David Davies project. Although considerable time was devoted to music and institute developments by a number of dedicated members, and its practical achievements were largely driven by Captain Jones and Burdon-Evans, it remained closely linked with David Davies and his sisters.

4: RESCUE AND CONSOLIDATION, 1924-39

The years from the early 1920s to the outbreak of war in 1939 were difficult times. To begin with, the Association faced an internal financial crisis that was not finally resolved until 1926. This had two immediate causes: the higher than expected cost of erecting temporary village institutes and the immense cost of the Pavilion that had been provided for the music festival. Both resulted from unanticipated rises in all costs associated with building – labour, materials and transport – especially in 1919-20, when the Association was pushing ahead with its construction programme. The same problem was encountered in housing and construction projects of all kinds across Britain.

The impact of this on the MCRA was twofold. Not only was outlay on construction higher than expected, but the contribution made by local associations to the MCRA was lower, as they too struggled with the higher costs. In most cases, local associations were to pay half the cost of their village institutes. Accounting records suggest that at least half were unable to contribute that proportion, with the result that the MCRA bore most of the cost.[1] The extra cost consumed the funds that had been intended for new work and more besides, leaving the Association with a substantial overdraft.

Financially, the final straw was the cost of the Pavilion. The urgency of finding a location may have exacerbated the rising building costs. The opportunity to buy a large aircraft hangar for £250 arose at short notice, at a time when there was some anxiety about the availability of a site for the festival. It was 'an apparently unparalleled bargain in semi-permanent buildings', as the annual report noted with some regret in 1922. It turned out to be no bargain. Tenders for the work of removal and re-erection seemed reasonable, but in the event were vastly exceeded. Haulage costs of so large a load from Lincoln were much higher than their estimates. Other factors included significant repairs and customization. The resulting building was considered very satisfactory as a venue, but it proved to be an enormous financial burden. Expecting costs to be substantially more than the outlay on the hangar, the Association obtained a loan of £2,000 for the purpose, but had to spend double that sum within a few months; the final cost was over £7,000.

The Association defended its decisions with the argument that real progress demanded that these developments should go ahead, but that as pioneers in the field they had no prior experience to draw on, simply advice from experts who were equally at sea in the new economic environment.[2] Attempts to attract more subscriptions and donations to fund this work met with little success. By 1926, the MCRA had an overdraft of over £8,900 – around £450,000 in 2019 terms.[3]

The MCRA was rescued by David Davies and his sisters, Margaret and Gwendoline, who proposed in 1924 to pay off the bank overdraft and permanently endow the association so that it would have a fixed income.[4] The following year, they made donations of £3,000 each, amounting to £9,000 in total. This cleared the overdraft,[5] and thereafter Gwendoline and Margaret Davies made annual donations sufficient to cover the cost of employing the secretary. [6] This rescue of the Association followed the Davies's approval of a reorganization scheme drawn up by Mr J. Tomley, who had been appointed secretary on a temporary basis for this purpose, and a small group of members. By the time this scheme was presented to the 1926 Annual General Meeting as consolidating the MCRA's most successful work and refocusing its future efforts, it was a *fait accompli*, and it had changed both the capacity of the Association and the nature of its work. The context in which the Association sought to make a difference was changing too. The threat of a general strike in Britain was looming in the mid-1920s, and the economic challenges facing the county had been mounting for some years.

The Impact of Reorganization

The volume of work carried out in the first two years of the MCRA's existence had fully occupied two secretaries and a Music Organizer, together with clerical assistance. That team directly organized leagues and other competitions in a range of sports, work that in football alone Captain Glynn Jones had reported taking up most of his time for several months, as well as a Sports Day, travelling cinema and lecture tours. Furthermore, the music festival and educational programme had been established. Local associations and village institutes had been set up all over the county.

Reorganization of the MCRA meant recognizing that this pioneering work was done. In particular, the institute network was declared complete. Captain Glynn Jones, who had driven that through, temporarily left for the south Wales coalfield after the 1921 coal strikes, a move that became permanent in 1923. With its capacity reduced, the MCRA's centrally organized activities were first pared back – some because they were unprofitable, others because they were deemed unnecessary – and the remainder were redefined as local work. This meant that lectures and educational programmes, for instance, would in future be organized by local recreation associations. These would be able to make arrangements directly with the YMCA or the Workers' Educational Association. Sports events and leagues would be run by free-standing county sports associations. The Association's role in county sport would be indirect. It would provide encouragement and publicity, as well as trophies and shields for leagues and other competitions, the latter allowing them a semblance of their former control in agreeing the rules of the competition for which a trophy was awarded.

The new arrangements meant there was no longer a Music Organizer. Although the amounts were not finalized until later, it was clear in 1924 that the generous income offered by the Davies family would not be enough to cover the salary and expenses of the Music Organizer. Consequently, the Association gave Mr Nicholas his notice that year. Captain Jones had already departed, and the following year the assistant secretary, Mr O. D. S. Taylor, resigned. A new secretary, Mr Edward Jones (formerly of the North Wales Village Clubs Association) was appointed in 1925 to a post that combined elements of the roles of secretary and Music Organizer, but at a lower salary. The new post did not include musical oversight, or conducting rehearsals and classes around the county, but it did involve organizing the festival and other musical activities, which now aimed to break even. Providing this could be achieved, and enough funds were raised from rents, fees and grants to cover usual expenses, both the Festival and the basic functions of the Association could be secured. Attaining this would take constant vigilance.

Music

The MCRA's Music and Eisteddfod committee adjusted itself to the new financial environment by acknowledging the need to break even. It combined that pressing reality with its ambitions to expand the audience for the music festival. It was well equipped to do so: it still had a large and very active cast of committee members and it had a Pavilion that was on the way to being fully fitted. Equally importantly, the festival itself continued to be presided over by Sir Walford Davies. This allowed it to build on its early success. Among the practices that seem to have contributed to a strong festival ethos, which perhaps compensated for the lack of a full-time music specialist, were the annual conferences of conductors and accompanists that were held at Gregynog, where Sir Walford's intentions were explained.

However, the festival was not free of problems. In April 1925, for instance, it faced the urgent need to find a conductor to take the place of Sir Walford, who had to withdraw on his doctor's orders. In the event, the festival went ahead in May as planned with Dr Adrian Boult as conductor. It was agreed that it was a success (apart from the disappointing finances), and the precaution was taken of inviting both conductors to take on the 1926 festival. The next year began with choirs making good progress, apart from two that would be absent: Churchstoke, because the men had deserted it for a male voice choir, and Llanbrynmair, which had no sopranos left. English choirs were rehearsing works in Welsh for the first time, and in April a massed rehearsal was conducted by Adrian Boult.

However, in early May 1926 the minutes express anxiety about the impact of the General Strike on the festival that was scheduled for later that month. On the advice of a contact at the Great Western Railway, the organizers held off postponing the festival. Choirs were warned to make alternative travel plans in case trains were not running and there were concerns about bookings drying up because of the uncertainty. The strike ended in time for the festival to go ahead on the scheduled date, but so widespread was the uncertainty that attendance and ticket sales were lower than expected, even after arranging for announcements to be made on the BBC that it was going ahead. The main beneficiaries of this were the County Schools, who got tickets at reduced prices as a result. In both cases, unexpected events were dealt with successfully at least in part because the organizers were already well aware that unanticipated decisions would need to be made at the last minute in live events, so a small 'emergency committee' was always authorized to do so.

However, in most years the problems were less dramatic than these. There were persistent concerns about maintaining the size and strength of the festival choir, and the participation or even existence of some choirs fluctuated. In 1934, the organizers noted how welcome it was to see the return of no less than eight choirs, while in 1935 the Knighton choir left to join the newly-formed Radnorshire festival. In 1937 the Corris choir was welcomed to the festival. The high standard of the festival choirs was a matter of great pride, and the secretary reported with satisfaction in 1934 that the 'casual chorister' had almost disappeared from their ranks.[7]

The festival continued to be successful in attracting prominent soloists and conductors. When in 1937 (the by then) Sir Adrian stepped down, he was replaced by Sir Henry Wood, who continued until 1939. The organizers of the festival were very well connected. Sir Walford was musical adviser to the BBC, whose Symphony Orchestra was conducted by Adrian Boult. Radio broadcasts from the festival are first mentioned in 1933, when the BBC broadcast part of the afternoon programme.[8] The minutes and correspondence of the Music and Festival committees rarely refer to the most influential connection of all, that with Gregynog, and not at all to the musical events held there by Gwendoline and Margaret Davies – choral concerts, then from 1933 to 1938 the Festival of Music and Poetry. But, of course, it was not necessary to mention this connection, as all present would be aware of the Davies's ability to draw prominent and influential musicians to Gregynog.[9]

The festival rarely met the injunction to break even, meaning that in most years it drew on the Association's dwindling reserves. The increasing concern of the Association's finance committee was not reflected in any significant reduction in the cost of orchestras and artists. The means adopted to increase income reflected the changing times. In the 1920s, there were frequent attempts – by Burdon-Evans and Colonel Harrison in particular – to raise more subscriptions and donations within the county, but this form of fundraising became less effective. Instead, as well as enlisting ticket agents to boost sales, the festival benefited from new sources of income, such as BBC fees and grants or guarantees from the Carnegie Trust (accessed by affiliating all choirs to the National Federation of Music Societies), which worked in conjunction with the National Council of Social Service. The same sources were successfully approached to subsidize conductors' classes, which gave further support to the work of festival choirs.[10]

Some aspects of the cherished music education became casualties of the new austerity, but only at the margins. In 1925, violin classes in the summer term were held at eight locations, with four (Berriew, Cemmaes, Caersws and Llanfyllin) as evening classes recognized by the County Education Authority. By autumn 1926, attendance had decreased in all areas and age groups, despite the provision being greatly appreciated by the remaining pupils. Owing to the fall in adult attendance only two evening classes could be recognized by the Authority, which reduced the grant and led to a financial loss. Nonetheless, although two classes were discontinued, the development of instrumental teaching and future orchestral talent was sufficiently important for the Association to persist with the scheme overall even though it rarely broke even. The Association was especially proud of another initiative designed to develop talent, the inaugural Newtown district

Children's Festival, held in 1925. It was successful musically and financially, and was held in the Pavilion. In 1928, this was held under the auspices of the county Education Authority, in conjunction with the MCRA, but although there are press references to the children's festival in the 1930s, there is no indication as to whether it was still held in partnership with the MCRA.[11]

Institutes, Centre and Locality

The MCRA's arrangements with local associations changed much more dramatically immediately after reorganization, and they continued to be adjusted for several years. The first issue was financial. Many of the local recreation associations were in debt to the MCRA as a result of having agreed to bear half of the cost of erecting the temporary village institutes. A few – such as Carno – escaped this problem, because the Association had borne the cost in full, thereby honouring a promise made by David Davies before the war, while Trefeglwys Institute was not funded by the MCRA at all. However, other local associations struggled to make repayments. Their financial position was reviewed during the reorganization by Mr Tomley, who concluded in 1926 that their struggle was a result of 'the very heavy cost of the Institutes which were erected when building prices were at their highest'.[12] Subsequently, a deflationary period of many years meant that not only did costs fall – too late to benefit the institute construction programme – but so did incomes. That made it even harder for local associations to raise money from the usual sources – membership, clubs, bazaars and donations – and meant that their original debts were now even more unaffordable. 'It was', reported Mr Tomley, 'obvious that the original arrangements could not be adhered to.'[13]

The MCRA agreed to reduce the amounts local associations should pay, and to accept payment over a longer period of time; in most cases the sums arrived at were agreed by the local association. Some did not need much assistance. For instance, Abermule paid all or most of its half-share within a few years, but many were in the same position as Caersws, whose target contribution was reduced by 70% to just £125 in 1926. By the time of the 1926 report, the sums actually received were still small, but it was hoped about £2,600 would be realized, sums that the Davies family had decided should be paid into a Reserve Fund to be utilized for other work.[14] Eventually most institutes paid back the revised amounts, some involving a further reduction in payments, but three local associations had still not managed to do so by 1932. By that stage, the Association had to write off more than half the loan to Guilsfield and one-third of that to New Mills.[15]

The revised funding arrangements were accompanied by a change in the nature of the relationship between county and local associations. A Local Association and Institute Conference organized by the MCRA was held in November 1926. The main theme of this was to affirm that the local associations were now responsible for all recreation, broadly defined, and that the County Association was anxious to support – rather than direct – them in this. It was also an opportunity to remind the local associations, and the public, of the importance of the work, and to provide 'an inspiration for all to persevere with the great task of making the institute a live centre for the welfare of all sections of the community'.[16]

The secretary reported the conviction that 'the future of village and Rural life depends upon the local Association ... and the Village Institute is the real centre of co-operation where all can meet free from distinction' of class or religion or 'where possible' of sex. Less positively, the secretary noted low levels of active membership in many places and the need to boost adolescent membership. But he singled out Sarn as a glowing example of what could be achieved, with eighty-six men and women of all ages, and all sections of the community actively involved. Finally, the conference report identified the need for outdoor space adjoining the Institutes. This was still not available everywhere and it was concluded that 'the Village Green is one of the pressing needs of today'. Clearly this need would not be met from the depleted Association funds, but supporting localities in finding ways of meeting it remained a key objective.

The Association continued to act as expert adviser where village halls or institutes were needed. The 1928 minutes give the example of the new Llanraiadr Village Hall, completed that year, which the MCRA had taken on the task of providing. It was noted that fundraising was so successful that it had been transferred to the local management free of debt. Most of the total cost of £3,333 had been raised from local efforts, and £600 was contributed by the Davies family. This was unusual. Although two years previously the Executive had echoed David Davies in emphasizing the temporary nature of the institutes, taking the view that each local association should already have a plan for getting and funding a permanent institute, few were able to do so in this period. One of those that did have such a plan, Llanfyllin, was advised by the MCRA in 1932 about making an application for a grant to the National Council for Social Service. The MCRA performed the same role for the Tregynon association in 1939.[17]

In many other localities associations carried on using the temporary institutes. The secretary could report in 1928 that they had successfully become the centre of many social activities, such as those of the Women's Institute, the Farmers' Union, the Guides, Scouts, choral societies, whist drives and dances. Only the low demand for the educational side of institute work was disappointing. This pattern continued. In the late 1930s, funding for physical activity became available through the National Fitness Council, and some local associations obtained substantial grants with the assistance of the MCRA's secretary.[18]

Dispensing with the old, autocratic, approach to local associations was seen as being beneficial to all parties. The Association reported in 1928 that the chairman's appeal to the local associations, made at the previous (1927) Annual Meeting, 'inviting them to appreciate the motto of the Association as being one which meant "To help, guide and further the interests of the local Associations rather than to dictate and control" has ... led to a better and happier relationship'.[19] Thereafter, institutes and local association business were much less prominent in the MCRA's minutes, but extensive correspondence between them and the secretary shows that the intention to maintain an advisory relationship was achieved and normalized.

Recreation Grounds and Funding

The need for more village greens that was highlighted at the Local Association conference of November 1926 makes it all the more surprising at first sight that in the following years the Association instituted a long programme of selling its recreation grounds. In 1930, part of the land held by the MCRA in Machynlleth was sold for £175.[20] More emblematic of the change in direction was the problem of the County Ground at Newtown. Since the abandonment of the County Sports Day, this ground had lost much of its purpose. Even the

Association minutes observed in 1928 that it had not achieved its early potential, becoming 'more or less the Newtown Recreation Ground'. Having tried adjusting rents and other plans, they sold the Ground to Newtown and Llanllwchaiarn Urban District Council in 1931 for £1,400 (£1,000 less than David Davies had paid for it in 1920).[21]

Subsequent sales of recreation grounds were mainly to local authorities or local associations. In 1932, Welshpool recreation ground was sold to Welshpool Town Council for £1,000, at the same time writing off all remaining debts of the Welshpool Recreation Association to the MCRA.[22] In 1934, the Association agreed to sell Newtown Football Ground in Pool Road to the trustees of Newtown Football Club for £450.[23] In 1938, Llandinam recreation ground was transferred to David Davies as partial repayment of a loan made by him to the MCRA. These were not the only examples. Between 1930 and 1938, most of the recreation grounds – three-quarters in terms of value – had been sold.[24]

A significant factor in the sale of the County Ground was the understanding that the district council should apply for a grant from the National Playing Fields Association to help with the purchase. The MCRA also stipulated that the district council should bear in mind its history of recreational use (a mild request considering that a stipulation of the original gift was that it should always be used for recreational purposes).[25] The Playing

Fields Association was also a voluntary or charitable trust, formed in 1925.[26] In 1930, the MCRA had invited its organizer to address a conference in order to learn more about membership and access its grants, so it may be that from this they formed the view that sale of the ground might allow the purchasers access to funding. In this case, however, it failed, and the MCRA itself made a grant to the council. Nonetheless the episode marks the beginning of the Association's involvement in a more institutional approach to fundraising. From this perspective, the sales of recreation grounds could be construed as a means of maximizing funding for achieving the MCRA's recreational objectives.

Sales of grounds also facilitated the MCRA's change in direction. In the same year as the sale of the Newtown Football Ground, it bought a property in Severn Place for £300. This was formerly Morgan's Wool Warehouse with an adjoining house. The MCRA converted it into offices and other accommodation for the YMCA and other community organizations in Newtown, when it became known as Community House.[27] The motive behind doing this was in part a response to another crisis: the Association was in urgent need of offices, as its tenancy of existing premises would expire in April 1934. The chairman, Burdon-Evans, had thus acted quickly when he found this building. It was a pragmatic response to an immediate difficulty that nonetheless led the Association towards a new means of supporting a broad spectrum of voluntary action.

Co-operation, Networks and the Voluntary System

The MCRA had active links with the wider voluntary movement from its early years. Since that time, the range of voluntary organizations active in Britain had grown and the National Council for Social Service played an increasingly important co-ordinating role, as well as being a source of grants for voluntary action, acting as an agent for the Development Commission. The National Council took the lead in promoting Rural Community Councils, and it offered financial help with setting them up, with the aid of funding from the Development Commission. When this initiative was formally launched in Wales in 1927, it was strongly supported by the MCRA.[28]

The Rural Community Councils were to have a consultative and co-ordinating role, fostering social facilities in order to combat depopulation. Their role was very similar to that envisaged by the founders of the MCRA. Indeed, the envisaged structure differed only in that it drew representatives from local authorities as well as from voluntary organizations. In practice, there was little difference on that count either, as some of the active MCRA committee members were also active in local government. Given the similarity of the proposed councils to its own structure, the MCRA may have seen no need for further action. It was not until 1931 that the Association convened a meeting about setting up a rural community council in Montgomeryshire,[29] after which it took a few months to draw up a 'scheme' (which is not reported in the minutes). In the autumn of 1932 the Association appointed Burdon-Evans as its representative to the newly-formed Montgomeryshire Community Council.[30] He became its chairman, while the MCRA's secretary, Edward Jones, became the council's honorary secretary.[31]

The relationship between the two is ambiguous in this period. On the face of it, these are two separate bodies. However, the same people were involved, suggesting the boundaries may have been unclear in practice. But Burdon-Evans was also involved in numerous other voluntary bodies, often as chairman. The same was true of the MCRA's chairman, Colonel Harrison. Activities attributed to the community council in press coverage, such as unemployment initiatives, are rarely recorded in MCRA executive or finance minutes, which mostly concentrate on property management or the music festival. But there is also no evidence of reports to or from the community council. Edward Jones travelled the county promoting local community councils and unemployment relief schemes in 1933, while he was employed full-time by the MCRA. Blurring the boundaries even further, the Association renamed its executive committee the 'Council'. A few years later, in 1937, the National Council for Social Services suggested the MCRA adopt 'Montgomery Community Council' as a subtitle, suggesting that there was by then no formally separate body after all and that the MCRA acted as the community council for the purposes of the National Council's structures.[32] Even so, this was not a settled arrangement. In 1939 the idea of the MCRA forming a new body was briefly revived, whether as a rural council or a voluntary sector umbrella body, but wartime priorities quickly moved beyond constitutions and subtitles, and neither idea was formally acted upon.

The surviving MCRA records do not support a fuller story of the early relationship between the two. It is hard to escape the – admittedly speculative – conclusion that the Rural Community Council represented an opportunity to relaunch the Association. With a new name and the backing of a national body it could distance itself from financial failures and resume the work of regenerating rural life, albeit in the very different context of the enforced leisure of unemployment. That this relaunch was in a different mode is clear from its reports in 1933, which highlighted four new activities. Two of these were attributed to other bodies: a drama bursary awarded by the National Council for Social Services and a drama school to be held in Newtown under the banner of the community council. The others were extra-mural classes, to be arranged in Llanfyllin, Newtown and Llanbrynmair, and the formation of a county table tennis league.[33] None of these were in any formal sense actions of the Association, but they were central to the MCRA's ideals. There is nothing remarkable about these reports, but they illustrate a shift towards the perspective of a consultative body rather than one directly engaged in running activities itself.

The Rural Community Council material in the MCRA collection highlights the many initiatives that were intended to combat mass unemployment during the 1930s. A representative example is the formation of a community council in Machynlleth in 1933, which included members of the local council, churches and chapels, the Recreation Association, Women's Institute, British Legion, school staff, medical practitioners, young people's associations and the unemployed themselves. The MCRA secretary explained that similar schemes in Newtown and Welshpool had asked the unemployed to submit schemes to the community council, since that without their help and consent nothing could be achieved. Many press reports of the time described self-help schemes for the unemployed, such as boot repair classes and access to allotments. In one case, the press reported two young Newtown men being sent on a short course at Coleg Harlech.[34]

Other bodies featured too. One example is the Montgomery County Advisory Committee for juvenile employment, which was set up under the auspices of the Ministry of Labour, and whose first meeting was presided over by Burdon-Evans. After explaining its purpose as aiming to help boys and girls to make employment choices by means of friendly supervision (a prototype of a careers service), he continued in terms reminiscent of his address to the MCRA inaugural meeting. He highlighted the need to help those struggling with the enforced leisure of unemployment to retain physical fitness and morale. Similar points were made at a benefit concert in aid of the National Council for Social Service, where he observed that there had been a remarkable awakening of the public conscience in the past few months, as shown by the rapid growth of small social work schemes. However, he also expressed the usual disappointment at the small amount of funds raised.[35]

Two years later, at the annual meeting of the MCRA in 1935, it was argued that there was still a need for a thorough survey of youth employment, which the MCRA would be best placed to take on. At the same time, the local Community Councils were working with the Workers' Educational Association to run '[I]ntellectual classes', including 'a course of lectures in Economics', while craft education classes (known as 'settlements') continued throughout the county and their produce was exhibited at Gregynog.[36]

A similar interweaving, but with more indication of the intended relationship between the parties, can be seen in an earlier scheme originating with Burdon-Evans. This was a plan to employ someone in connection with the Welsh-language music magazine *Y Cerddor* and the Robert Owen Museum. The detail is unclear, in part because the MCRA hosted the project without taking responsibility for it. Work was supervised by the secretary (who was also involved with the museum) and payment was routed via the Association bank account.[37] Burdon-Evans had also been responsible for the Association agreeing to act as a county branch of the Society for the Preservation of Rural Wales in 1930.[38] He would later be instrumental in the Association hosting a Rural Industries regional organizer covering the counties of Montgomeryshire and Radnorshire, which after some negotiation was finally agreed in 1939. This was another scheme funded by the Development Commission, through the Rural Industries Bureau, to improve skills among the rural workforce. Such repetition of the practices of hosting, interweaving and consultation suggest a deliberate approach to influencing and the execution of social work.

The Gregynog Network

Connections between the Music Festival and the interests and musical activities of Gwendoline and Margaret Davies were far from being the only ways in which the Gregynog network influenced the MCRA, especially after the financial rescue of the organization was completed in 1926.

Alongside their cultural and artistic mission, the sisters held conferences on social as well as musical matters at Gregynog, especially bringing together those concerned with the National Council for Social Service in Wales, many of whom were influential in other ways. Burdon-Evans was among those who took part in these conferences – along with, for instance, Sir Walford Davies and Sir Percy Watkins, who became head of the new Welsh division of the National Council for Social Service in 1933. Another link in this network was the former Cabinet Secretary, Thomas Jones, founder of Coleg Harlech and supporter of the Workers' Educational Association and adult education in general. In 1930 he became secretary of the Pilgrim Trust, with close links to the Carnegie Trust (from which the Music Festival obtained grants that offset its losses). Youth work was discussed at Gregynog conferences too, bringing Captain Glynn Jones back to Montgomeryshire for discussions of boys and girls clubs, and later as Welsh Organizer of the National Fitness Council.

The direction taken by the MCRA in the 1930s is very close to the concerns of these advocates, and of delegates to a social service conference at Gregynog in 1933 in particular. The Association may have become aware of the changing nature of grant-funding available to social services through these contacts.[39] The concern expressed in this circle for adult education and training as a means of social reconstruction also informed the MCRA's practical initiatives, such as the Association's successful bid to act as a Rural Industries Centre.

Transition

The days of glowing, even gushing, press coverage of the Association itself were over by the 1930s. It no longer claimed the dominant voice in recreational matters that had characterized its earlier approach. Grounds were sold, sporting and intellectual activities were left in the hands of local and specialist associations, and the MCRA no longer took on headline-grabbing events such as the sports day. With this change, participation declined: the MCRA was initially an association in which the committee structure was also a participation structure, and without the many sports committees, broad participation in the life of the Association itself declined. Its management lay in the hands of small numbers of indefatigable individuals, while attendance at AGMs amounted to perhaps twelve people or fewer. This was countered by the thriving music network, which maintained participation from across the county through choirs.

In other ways, too, the Association retained a greater presence than its formal actions suggest. Its secretary was active in many such activities behind the scenes, advising or even organizing on behalf of such bodies as the Community Councils, and the chairman and other prominent members did likewise. The network of choirs, local and sports associations had become normal, rather than a novelty, and the institutes were a visible token of that new normality. The period also marked a transition from the early attempts to found action on donations from prominent county families, to which few responded to the degree necessary, to the more modern fundraising practices of seeking grants from large foundations and government agencies. In the process, they gained insight and undoubtedly advice through the excellent networks that Gwendoline and Margaret Davies, with their brother, assembled at Gregynog.

The times were in all other respects far from normal, of course, and the Association's original concerns about the proper use of leisure took a new shape in the face of the enforced leisure of mass unemployment. The declaration of war, again, in 1939 brought this transitional phase to an abrupt close.

5: WAR AND MODERNIZATION, 1939-82

Following the outbreak of war in 1939 the County Music Festival was halted and attempts to create new social work schemes were paused. Little else is known about the MCRA's wartime activity. After six years in which all activity took second place to the war effort, the Association emerged from the conflict into a new social order. The Education Act of 1944, in particular, would see the state taking responsibility for provision of such facilities as playing fields and further education. In the next thirty years the MCRA disposed of most of its remaining grounds and village halls, sold the County Pavilion and was forced to sell Community House at Newtown. It concentrated on its work as a community council, which meant supporting a range of voluntary organizations and parish councils, as well as its long-standing work with the music festival. In this work, it was increasingly supported by grants from government agencies, which left it vulnerable to the changes in government policy that took place in the 1960s and 1970s. Of these, the most dramatic in its effect on the MCRA was the creation in 1975 of a combined rural council for the new county of Powys. This left the MCRA without the role it had played for over forty years. It was uncertain what part – if any – it would play in the future.

The War and its Aftermath

War brought loss: within two weeks of the declaration of hostilities, minutes recorded condolences to Canon Bell, a longstanding member, on the death in action of his only son.[1] After that, the MCRA records are in the main silent on the privations and losses of war, although a few indications of its impact can be gleaned. Community House, in Severn Place, and the County Pavilion were requisitioned for military use, and the 1940 County Music Festival was cancelled soon afterwards. Several of the choirs decided to carry on rehearsing the chosen music, despite the knowledge that there would be no opportunity to form a massed choir. Instead, they gave local concerts in aid of war charities. Some concerts were given in village institutes, which became locations for morale-boosting activities that were encouraged by the authorities.[2]

Institutes also became venues for activity that was more directly associated with the war effort, as correspondence between the MCRA and Arddleen Recreation Association illustrates. The local recreation association had been in correspondence with the Home Guard during the war, and this ended with the Arddleen association reluctantly agreeing to halve the usual charges for use of the Institute. This seems not to have damaged its relations with the local Home Guard, for in January 1945 the secretary of Arddleen recreation association wrote:

> *At a committee last week, the Home Guard asked for the hire of the room for a Home Guard supper with permission for free beer to drink the toasts. Some members thought it was against the rules to drink beer in the Institute ... Being as it is the stand down supper the committee agree to allow the beer into the Institute if the Recreation Association have no rule against it ... I understand a number of Institutes have allowed it.*[3]

The reply from the MCRA (29 January 1945) had bad news for the Home Guard: 'I have to inform you that the rule "No intoxicants of any kind be allowed on the premises" applies to all Institutes affiliated to the Association … it is not possible or advisable to make an exception at the present time.'[4]

Correspondence with several local associations concerning insurance or management matters indicates that most institutes at least ticked over during the war years. Similar correspondence continued for many years afterwards. The Arddleen local association kept the MCRA's secretary particularly busy. For instance, in 1947 the local committee anxiously asked whether it would be allowed to hire the hall to a mobile cinema being run by two young ex-servicemen, and it was especially anxious to stress that the men were doing so to make a living.[5] This time it got a positive response from the MCRA.

The End of an Era

Lord Davies died on 16 June 1944. The last wartime annual meeting of the MCRA recorded not only this grievous loss, but also the end of an era. The Association paid tribute to Lord Davies and to the 'inestimable services rendered by him to the Association, to Montgomeryshire and to Wales'.[6] It also mourned the death in action in the same year of his son, the second Lord Davies. The same meeting moved on to regret the loss to music and the Association occasioned by the deaths of the conductors Sir Walford Davies (11 March 1941) and Sir Henry Wood (19 August 1944). Sir Walford was the founder and president of the County Music Festival. As the guiding spirit behind its music scheme, he was much missed by the festival organizers. But with the death of David Davies, the MCRA had lost its founder and its inspiration.

Most of the post-war officers of the MCRA had worked with, or for, David Davies throughout the Association's existence, and his ideas continued to guide their ambitions for the organization. But they were getting old and tired. In 1946, Burdon-Evans confessed to profound disillusionment over the failure of several causes he had believed in, and by now he was exhausted.[7] In the following years, MCRA meetings paid tribute to many of this band of men who had been loyal to voluntary action in the county. Edward Jones, the long-serving secretary of the Association, died in 1948, while W. E.

Pryce Jones and Burdon-Evans followed in 1949. There were many others. When a new village hall was opened by the Hon. Mary Davies at Carno in 1949, it was the occasion for tributes to that generation. One such was the late Edward Jones, who was warmly praised for his efforts to replace the hall after its destruction by fire eleven years previously. Colonel Harrison took the opportunity to speak appreciatively of the life's work of the late Lord Davies and the inspiration he provided.[8]

A New Era and a New Generation

The context in which the MCRA operated was undergoing rapid change. After the 1945 general election, the British state was re-invented. The 'welfare state' took on responsibilities for health, education and other aspects of welfare. Some of the functions of the pre-war Association now seemed less crucial. For instance, local education authorities would now be responsible for much of the educational work the Association had promoted. The creation of the National Health Service did not directly affect the Association, but it is possible that it had an indirect impact by reducing the need for voluntary fund-raising that attempted to support hospitals under the previous system.

The mass unemployment that disfigured the 1930s was no longer a significant problem, but successive governments became more active in schemes to develop the rural economy. One of the ways in which it did so was by increasing the funding work to improve rural skills through the Rural Industries Bureau. The MCRA became involved in this initiative in 1939, but after the war it became a more significant part of the MCRA's activity, when a new rural industries organizer was recruited by the Association to a post funded by grants from the Development Commission. The work mainly involved training in skills that were deemed necessary to industries and craftsmen that supported agriculture. In the 1930s, this had meant training wheelwrights, but in the 1950s the greatest demand was for skills in oxy-acetylene welding. As an agent of the Bureau, the MCRA supervised the organizer, whose work covered three counties (including Montgomeryshire), but it had little scope to direct the nature of the work.

The Development Commission also became more involved in attempts to stem the accelerating rate of rural depopulation. It did this through a programme intended to provide social facilities, which in some respects corresponded to both the plans set out by David Davies some forty years earlier and the aims and objectives of the MCRA. For instance, central funds were made available for village halls, which were administered through the National Council of Social Services. In turn, this council gave grants, advice and instructions to Rural Community Councils (which were unelected organizations, and are not to be confused with the elected community councils of the late twentieth century). It was a very hierarchical structure. Acting in the role of a rural community council, the MCRA continued to advise local associations and other village hall committees about all sorts of matters. The most significant of these was obtaining grants for new or replacement village halls, which became a realistic prospect once government restrictions on materials were lifted in the 1950s. Correspondence from this period suggests that two different cultures met in the Association's in-tray. One culture is represented by the discursive, and sometimes elaborately courteous, handwritten letters of local secretaries who sought advice and grants. These are in sharp contrast to another culture of cursory and impersonal missives from the central offices of the National Council. Perhaps it is just as well there was a county secretary to mediate between these two worlds.

The Development Commission, as the funding body, defined the role of Rural Community Councils more closely in the early 1950s. The result was a long and challenging list of responsibilities, from promoting a prototype citizens' advice bureau to the provision of welfare services (such as services to the elderly) on behalf of local authorities. Providing administrative services for local organizations was also part of the brief.[9] It is around this time that the MCRA began to use the sub-title 'Montgomery Rural Community Council' in its internal documents, which report activity under headings that correspond to the Commission's list of responsibilities. Secretarial services were supplied to, among others, the Playing Fields Association, the Parish Councils Association and the Powys Fine Art Association. The County Best-Kept Village Competition also featured, along with flower shows. The social welfare aspect of Community Council work was represented in the MCRA's work through groups dealing with 'Old People's Welfare' for instance, or the organization of chiropody services. In all these ways the MCRA carried out work that corresponded with that of other rural community councils in Wales.

Alongside these activities, the MCRA continued to run the County Music Festival, as well as the recently formed Mid-Wales Orchestra. Unlike the voluntary groups that it supported organizationally, these were constituent parts of the MCRA, which was very proud that the Music Festival remained an annual event. The local education authority now employed a County Music Organizer, who acted as the festival chorus master, so the festival was nonetheless becoming a more collaborative exercise. It also obtained increasing levels of Arts Council grants towards the inevitable financial loss it incurred.[10] From 1952, the Arts Council guarantee of financial backing was obtained on condition that a full professional orchestra was employed. When the Liverpool Philharmonic Orchestra played at the festival for the first time in May 1952, the MCRA proudly claimed that it was the first time that a full professional orchestra had played in the county.[11] The Music

Committee that ran the festival adopted a separate constitution in 1961, which allowed it to join the Standing Conference of Amateur Music but it did not intend to sever its ties with the MCRA.[12]

The MCRA still owned property that supported these in-house activities. The County Pavilion needed improvement by the 1950s, but it was still well-used and there were plans to make it more suitable for drama and operatic performances. Community House, in Severn Place, Newtown, was requisitioned for longer and not until 1951 could the Association look forward to finally regaining access to the building.[13] Once it did so, it was let to voluntary sector and statutory organizations and was used as a venue for small meetings and exhibitions. In the 1950s the MCRA still owned some recreation grounds outside Newtown, a few of which were retained until almost the end of the century. In these respects, the MCRA retained a small core of inherited activity that did not correspond to the normal work of a rural community council.

In the process, the MCRA began to modernize. In 1950, it adopted a new constitution and elected as its president the young Hon. Islwyn Davies, one of Lord Davies's sons. It was now a limited company and a registered charity, which were considered more suitable for the modern world than the previous arrangements. Its objects were simplified, to highlight support for other voluntary organizations and causes. Although the directly-organized activities of its earlier years were not ruled out by the new constitution, they were less prominent. Those activities would be supported through relationships with other voluntary groups. Its new constitution also signalled a move away from voluntarism, as it would now specifically offer places on its council to representatives of local authorities as well as of voluntary organizations.[14]

The modern MCRA had been redesigned as a Rural Community Council in all but name. Like all other rural community councils, it was a member of the National Council of Social Services, and its activities were consistent with their guidance or, increasingly, their direction. That allowed it to be part of a wider movement, one that gave it the opportunity to obtain grants from government or from the National Council, but which came at the expense of independence. That may have been inevitable. By the 1950s the MCRA no longer had the means to act as an independent pioneer organization, since the annual contribution from the Davies sisters' trust had declined significantly in real terms and could contribute only a portion of its administrative costs.[15] Thus, the MCRA's new role was carved out in the spaces left to voluntary work by the still-developing welfare state.

The Impact of the Modernizing State

The MCRA had established its role more firmly by the 1950s, but in the process it had become more vulnerable to changes in government policy and structures. In the 1960s, economic development priorities changed. The Rural Industries initiatives that had been distributed among the MCRA and similar bodies were merged in 1968 into a new agency, the Council for Small Industries in Rural Areas (which, the MCRA commented, was hardly a snappy title). The new body ran its programme in-house, so the MCRA lost its funding for rural industries and with it the means to employ an organizer. After a transitional period as an observer of the new arrangements, the MCRA had no further involvement other than to rent offices in Community House to the new body.

More fundamental changes followed. When local government in Wales was re-organized with effect from 1 April 1974, Montgomeryshire became one of three components of the new county of Powys, along with Radnorshire and Breconshire. The former county was now represented by Montgomery District Council (which was later renamed Montgomeryshire, despite remaining a second tier district council). A new Development Board for Rural Wales replaced the previous Development Corporation. It covered a large tract of rural Wales, including all of Powys, and because it had both a social and an economic development remit its decisions would shape a great deal of the policy environment that the MCRA now had to navigate. Meanwhile, ultimate power over such development in Wales passed from the Development Commission to the Welsh Office. The modernization of the State had completely changed the context in which the MCRA operated.

The MCRA had to adapt to even greater challenge than the changed structures of the State and its agencies. While these plans were being laid, a similar amalgamation took place between the rural community councils of the three counties, which in 1975 were replaced by a new entity, Powys Rural Council.[16] This change was preceded by three years in which a co-ordinating committee made up of representatives of the three rural community councils gradually prepared the way for a shadow council in 1974, prior to the new body taking over on 1 April 1975.[17] The MCRA lost all of its rural council functions to the new body. That meant it no longer received a grant for this work and so no funding for the staff it previously employed. Its secretary departed to become chief officer of the new rural council, and advised the MCRA that it needed to give serious consideration to its future role.[18] It began an arrangement with the Powys Rural Council that continued until 2001, under which it paid an agency fee for administrative support, which ensured that for a few years there was some continuity in handling its affairs.

Plans laid by the Association in this period envisaged a future as a grant-awarding charity, and it identified two broad areas it aimed to support with grants – outward-bound scholarships and small voluntary projects in the Montgomery district.[19] These aims varied a little in practice; for example, in 1976 it earmarked £300 per year for educational exchange schemes, and in 1980 it gave a grant of £1,000 to aid the development of an outward-bound centre at Staylittle.[20] The MCRA's operating income was by now negligible, so this support was funded from the return on its investments. In turn, this derived mainly from the proceeds of the sale of two properties in Newtown, which took place in 1974.

Lost Property: Community House and the Pavilion

The Association's capacity to offer practical support to both community and cultural activities was drastically reduced by the sale of Community House and the County Pavilion. In 1964 both buildings had played a large part in accommodating the National Eisteddfod when it was hosted by Newtown, and both were thronged with visitors throughout the week. Ten years later things had changed.

Community House was in need of serious repairs and maintenance, and it no longer generated enough income to cover the cost of a full-time administrator. Improvements to the property were considered, but in

1974 it was subject to a compulsory purchase order to make way for a new road system in Newtown. There is no record of any discussions about the Association seeking alternative premises, and the proceeds from the forced sale were instead invested, following negotiation with the Charity Commission.[21] In the process, the nature of the Association's support for voluntary groups was changed significantly.

At the end of the 1960s, the Pavilion was no longer the well-used building it had been at the start of the decade. Its lack of modern amenities was no longer acceptable, but because the structure had deteriorated to the point of being unsafe, professional advice was that there was nothing to be gained by spending money on improvements.[22] In 1970, the MCRA began the process of finding ways to replace it. Consultations with local authorities and the development board took place in 1971, and although the MCRA and the town council both wanted a general-purpose hall and swimming pool to be built on the site, it became clear that it would be too expensive in the financial circumstances under which local authorities operated.[23] A sports hall and swimming pool seemed the best compromise, and in 1974 the MCRA sold the Pavilion to Newtown and Llanllwchaiarn Urban District Council for this purpose.[24] That should have been the end of the matter: demolition of the Pavilion would be the end of another era in the Association's history but one with the consolation that something had been achieved for the town. Instead, the MCRA became embroiled in a long battle over the charitable purposes for which the land was given in the first place.

The problem began when Montgomery District Council (to whom the site passed on re-organization of local government) decided to build the sports centre at Newtown High School instead. As the council no longer needed the Pavilion site, it proposed selling it. That was a cause for concern to the MCRA, owing to the history and charitable status of the site. It had been bought for the County Pavilion through a public subscription in Newtown in the 1920s, which raised £410, and it had been transferred to the MCRA in 1925 under a charitable trust. The terms of this trust deed account for the curious fact that, before it could sell the land to the council, the MCRA first had to pay the same council the sum that had been raised by subscription in the first place (as a proxy for the original subscribers).[25] Every subsequent change in ownership or purpose would be framed by the law of trusts, which by this time meant, in practice, obtaining permission from the Charity Commission on each occasion.

Aerial view of the County Pavilion

A few years after the sale the MCRA expressed disquiet that the site was not being used.[26] It was also dismayed at the district council's preference for selling the land for housing and using the proceeds to subsidize the sports hall. This concern was one it shared with the town council, as it would end the dream of developing a new general-purpose hall on the site.[27] The MCRA was especially outraged because it had inserted a restrictive covenant in the deeds specifically prohibiting such a sale. To add to the injury, it had accepted a low price on that basis and feared that a vast profit was being made at its expense.[28] The MCRA maintained a long and deeply frustrated correspondence with both the district council and the Charity Commission on this theme for several more years. Twice it suggested that if the land had to be sold and the proceeds placed in trust the MCRA should act as the trustee. From the MCRA's perspective, this would have restored the purpose of the original bequest.

The eventual outcome was very disappointing for the MCRA. Its arguments had probably contributed to the Commission dropping its first plan, which would have allowed the council to retain the proceeds of the sale, but it failed to regain control of the trust. The land was sold at market valuation for housing, and the 'profit' (the proceeds less the amount already paid to the MCRA) was vested in a charitable trust, the Montgomery District Trust Fund.[29] Both the District Council and the Charity Commission rejected the MCRA's request to become the trustee, and the council chose to act as trustees themselves. [30]

Beyond the legal arguments, the episode touched on the identity of the MCRA. Very little was known about the MCRA's origins at the time, beyond the year of its formation, and the original constitution could not be identified with any certainty. As the meaning of 'recreation' changed over time, the full intentions of the founders were no longer as obvious as they once were. It may be that this contributed to the ensuing difficulties in communicating the Association's objects. The MCRA had first agreed to a narrow interpretation of recreation being applied to the site; then it found itself debarred from regaining control of the resulting trust because its own objects were much broader.[31]

Seeking a New Role

Most playing fields and village institutes that had remained in MRCA ownership until the 1950s were subsequently transferred to local associations or councils, and these transactions were far less troublesome. In most cases, the transfers allowed village hall associations to become independent and to apply for funds to renew or modernize their halls, aims which were wholly consistent with the MCRA village institute programme when it began in 1920. These disposals did not pose a threat to the MCRA or to its ideals.

The saga of the Montgomery District Trust Fund, in which the MCRA finally admitted defeat in 1982, was more damaging.[32] The impact of a disappointing outcome was exacerbated not only by the manner of the proceedings, but also by their timing. The failure to regain control of those charitable funds, with the accompanying failure to secure the general-purpose hall they had sought, occurred soon after the compulsory purchase of Community House, and after the equally unsought loss of the rural council role on which it had focused for over forty years. In the new world of interventionist government agencies, a small, shrinking charity could expect to have little influence. In the end, it accepted that at best it could play an advisory role to the District council, a role that was negotiated through the local MP, Alex Carlile.[33] By 1990, the MCRA seemed sufficiently reconciled to these new circumstances to note in its annual report that it had advised thirty-one applicants to the Montgomery District Trust Fund. It expressed pleasure that this fund, one that was very important to voluntary organizations in the county, was so well publicized by the district council.

That the MCRA was still in a position to make such encouraging comments, rather than having accepted demotion to the ranks of small and little-known charities, is due to one other development that took place in this period – the establishment of the Davies Memorial Gallery in Newtown. This is discussed in the next chapter.

6: ART AND THE COMMUNITY, 1967-2019

The MCRA's connection with the visual arts began much later than its connection with music. Its long, and sometimes troublesome, involvement with providing an exhibition space for the visual arts and crafts in Montgomeryshire began in earnest in 1967 with the opening of the Davies Memorial Gallery in Newtown. After this, the nature of the MCRA's role in supporting the visual arts changed more than once. At first, the building was run by the MCRA as a combined community centre and gallery, where art classes and the volunteers who ran the visual arts programme in the building shared the exhibition space with choirs and other community groups. This became more difficult once the MCRA lost its Community Council functions in 1975, and the staff that went with them. A second phase can be dated to 1985, when the MCRA began its association with Oriel 31, a professional gallery based in Welshpool.

The third phase saw the Davies Memorial Gallery completely reconfigured in the early years of the twenty-first century, when it was transformed into a dedicated visual arts venue. This is the defining development in the history of the MCRA in this period, not only because of the high standard of the venue itself but also because it was only made possible by the acquisition of alternative premises for the community groups that had previously shared the gallery space. In turn, this meant that as it reached its centenary the MCRA could once again support both community work and cultural activities.

Antecedents: Welshpool and Newtown

Although the Memorial Gallery was a new departure, it was not the first time the MCRA had been involved with visual art. The MCRA had provided administrative support to the Powys Fine Art Association from 1953 until at least 1965. This association had access to an exhibition venue in Welshpool, which was the main focus of its activity. In this period, the Arts Council and major museums provided a list of touring exhibitions from which smaller venues could make their choice of programme. As the Fine Art Association became more established, it put great effort into acquiring exhibitions for long enough to show in both Welshpool and Newtown, and to have exhibitions on display in both locations at the same time.[1] This was difficult to achieve. The most valuable or delicate exhibits required security, lighting and environmental standards that limited where they could be shown, and no suitable venues were available in Newtown or in the rest of the county. This is demonstrated most clearly by an Arts Council touring exhibition in Welshpool in 1965 that was probably the most valuable and certainly the most newsworthy of all those it had seen: a selection of one hundred original works from the collection of the late

Margaret Davies. The exhibition included works by two renowned Welsh painters, Augustus John and Ceri Richards, and it generated widespread press attention.[2] In the next two years it toured to cities across Britain, but despite is connections to the county, there is no record of it being shown in any other venue in Montgomeryshire.

A second motivation may have been the increasing struggle experienced by the Fine Art Association. It was difficult to break even, even with a modest Arts Council grant. In good years, this association could employ a caretaker or attendant to ensure regular opening hours, but later it had to rely on volunteers for all aspects of its work. By 1963, the ageing volunteers were complaining of finding the work of unpacking and hanging exhibitions far too laborious.[3] Then in 1965 it faced the unwelcome news that it would lose the Welshpool venue at the end of the year, when it would be taken over by the County Library service.

The Memorial Gallery

It is Gwendoline and Margaret Davies's outstanding legacy and lifetime gifts of paintings, sculptures and other artworks that are most clearly celebrated by the decision to construct a gallery as a memorial to them. It was another of the sisters' legacies that enabled the construction of the building, in particular the charitable trust Margaret had established in the 1930s in response to the distressing hardship and social need of that period. After the death of Margaret Davies in 1963, her nephew, the Hon. Islwyn Davies, together with his sister-in-law Lady Davies, agreed there should be a memorial to both sisters' life and work, and as trustees of the Gwendoline and Margaret Davies charities they took the decision that these trusts would fund it.[4] The decision is not documented in any detail in the MCRA records. The MCRA simply welcomed the news, which was announced to its council in June 1965, that the trustees proposed erecting a building in memory of the sisters.[5] The proposal, at that point in its initial stages, was that it would include an exhibition hall, a conference room and offices for the MCRA. The final design conceived these three elements as separate blocks, so that each could be used independently. It was envisaged that the gallery block, the largest of the three, should also be multifunctional, able to house concerts as well as exhibitions, and the architects took care to consult the Arts Council on its design.[6]

No more is said about this building in the MCRA records until after it moved into the new offices in the building in 1967.There was far more coverage in the press across Britain. The *Birmingham Daily Post*, for instance, reported that plans were being made to erect the memorial gallery and that the district council was seeking approval to hand over a site in the town park for this purpose.[7] The site, a small area of the park at Newtown Hall, was acquired by the MCRA on a 100-

year lease at a token rent.[8] Two years later, the *Post's* Welshpool correspondent took an unkindly swipe at the architecture of the new gallery. Neither the architect nor the district council was deterred by criticism, which had already circulated locally, of its modern 'box-like' style. The building was designed by Alan Roberts of the Alex Gordon Partnership in Cardiff, known for its pioneering approach to sustainable architecture.[9] He reminded critics that it was 1967 not 1867: the building was intended to be modern. Two years later it was recognized with a Civic Trust award.[10] By the 1990s it had become part of the furniture and it was regarded as 'visually quiet and unassuming'.[11]

THE

GWENDOLINE AND MARGARET DAVIES

MEMORIAL GALLERY

Opened by

SIR BEN BOWEN THOMAS, M.A., LL.D.

on

SATURDAY, 28th OCTOBER, 1967

Souvenir programme (Courtesy of the Hon. Mrs Camilla Davies).

The Davies Memorial Gallery was officially opened on 28 October 1967 by Sir Ben Bowen Thomas.[12] Two weeks earlier, the MCRA moved out of Community House to offices in the new building, taking the Darby and Joan club and a few other social functions with them. Community House continued to be let to social groups, adding the Youth Hostel Association to its list of tenants. The opening exhibition showed the personal and the public art that the sisters had lived with – over forty paintings by Gwendoline, as well as fourteen works from the collection donated by the Davies sisters to the National Museum of Wales. This combination set the tone of the early years of the art gallery. In November 1967, following a public meeting, the MCRA formed a new County Arts Committee.[13] Its aim was to find ways of broadening the reach of this work and to find new members, so that it avoided the narrow geographical focus of the former Powys Fine Arts Association.[14] How successful it was in that aim is unclear, but it did at first benefit from the experience of the Welshpool group, and one of those, Mr Bret Jehu, later became a president of the MCRA. There were art classes, organized by MCRA staff in collaboration with the extra-mural department at the University College of Wales, Aberystwyth. A full exhibition programme for 1968-9 was arranged with the assistance of the Welsh Arts Council, which also advised on how to make best use of the building.[15]

Like the Powys Fine Art Association, the new organization exhibited work from art classes as well as touring museum exhibitions. For instance, in the last three months of 1969 exhibitions included 'Paintings and Drawings from the Arts Council of Great Britain collection', 'Wales Now', an exhibition drawn from a

'Youth and the Arts' week arranged in co-operation with the education authority, and the Mid-Wales New Town Corporation exhibition.[16] In 1970-1 there were only seven exhibitions, including the work of art classes and local groups, all with a Welsh theme. At the same time, the Memorial Gallery was in great demand for meetings and other events, which were dominated by groups based in Newtown. The work necessary to put on and supervise exhibitions was carried out almost entirely by volunteers. In these circumstances it seems inevitable that in practice the volunteers would be mainly drawn from nearby, and the Memorial Gallery would become a local rather than a county facility.

After 1975, this approach became more difficult to sustain. The art committee became just one of the many community groups using the building, and the MCRA welcomed the income provided by community group rents. For several years, the gallery running costs were subsidized by investment income, which the MCRA had intended to use to make grants to the community. In the meantime, exhibitions continued, but they appear to have been relatively small in scale and varied a lot in number. For instance, in 1980 there were eight exhibitions, while in the following year there were only four, and more of those were touring exhibitions. At some point in the late 1970s the MCRA rejected an unspecified suggestion by the Arts Council on the grounds that it was too expensive and too complicated. Some years later, it was more ambitious. In 1984 it applied for Arts Council funding, which would allow it to upgrade the gallery to accommodate 'grade A' exhibitions and to employ an exhibitions officer. That bid was not successful; the scheme had been shelved owing to insufficient Arts Council funds.[17] It also seems to have coincided with a change in the Arts Council's priorities, which became less welcoming to mixed-use spaces. While the community centre aspect of the Memorial Gallery was thriving, the MCRA had more difficulty finding the means to promote the gallery as an arts venue.

Oriel 31 at the Memorial Galley

A new approach to visual arts at the Memorial Gallery came from Welshpool, in the form of a proposal to the MCRA from Oriel 31. This was a small gallery set up in 1982 on Welshpool's High Street. Its founding directors (Elaine Marshall, Sophie Meade and Michael Nixon) proposed taking over the exhibition facilities to create a new gallery called 'Oriel at the Memorial'. This would be a professional full-time exhibition centre run in conjunction with the Welsh Arts Council and the Aberystwyth Arts Centre. The MCRA was in favour of the idea, as it would at last create a fully professional gallery in the building.[18] The cost of preparing the gallery space was shared between them, and 'Oriel at the Memorial' took up residence in the Memorial Gallery late in 1985.[19]

The directors of Oriel 31 were ambitious for the new venture. They emphasized that their small Welshpool venue had succeeded in attracting 6,000 visitors to its exhibitions and craft displays, not to mention funding from the Arts Council, the Craft Council and other sources. The directors were confident that in the much larger, purpose-built space of the Davies Memorial Gallery, with its excellent access and more populated hinterland, they could establish a highly successful centre for the arts in mid-Wales. Although they would retain their Welshpool gallery, one of the directors would be based in Newtown, and Oriel 31 would undertake the necessary fundraising. Their proposal set out the programme they intended to run in 1985-6, starting with a landscape exhibition featuring the work of artists Peter Prendergast, Mary Lloyd Jones, Roy Able and others, as well as an exhibition of 'Outsider Art', loan and touring exhibitions, and a range of other craft and art displays.

Oriel 31's proposal also claimed that the Welshpool gallery had a strong community base, with the implication that it would seek to replicate that in Newtown. This would be an important feature of the venture from the MCRA perspective, since the building continued to house a range of community group meetings and activities. But the proposal suggests that MCRA and Oriel 31 had divergent ideas about the meaning of community activity. Oriel 31 classed the life drawing and other art classes that it ran as community engagement, along with poetry readings and lectures. It also relied on a large and enthusiastic team of volunteers to staff the Welshpool gallery and it intended to do the same in Newtown. Even so, there was some concern about which other activities would share the space. For instance, while Oriel 31 wanted the Severnside Art Group to be part of the programme, choir rehearsals in the exhibition space were less welcome because they were seemingly a risk to the exhibits. Other community groups, such as the Women's Institute and the Darby and Joan club, posed no risk as they would continue to use a separate block of the building.

The MCRA was very pleased with the new arrangements. Oriel 31 had been selected by the Welsh Arts Council to be one of a small number of galleries to receive development funding. The exhibitions put on by Oriel were popular and they attracted a growing number of visitors. This brought the Davies Memorial Gallery to wider attention, and it was hoped that this would bring more attention to the MCRA.[20] The success of the gallery was attributed 'to the foresight and endeavour' of Michael Nixon, the gallery's director, and the trustees of Oriel 31, one of whom had joined the MCRA's council.[21] The MCRA had good reason to be pleased, as its dual-purpose building now housed the two strands of activity it was designed for, which were managed and staffed by two separate, focused organizations – Oriel 31 and the Rural Community Council.

It did not take long for the limitations of this arrangement to become apparent. There was not enough space available for the full gallery operation they envisaged – especially for offices and stores, and a separate craft display area. Their directors argued that their success in rapidly increasing the number of visitors exacerbated the problem.[22] When the tenancy came up for renewal in 1989, Oriel 31 and the MCRA nonetheless agreed another. In spite of these shortcomings, the MCRA reported that the exhibitions attracted over twenty thousand visitors in 1989-90.[23]

Oriel 31 had bigger plans. In 1989 and 1990 it drew up two plans for extending the gallery space. The first envisaged a small extension at a somewhat optimistic cost of £20,000.[24] The second involved more interior re-modelling of the building, as well as an extension, at a cost of £80,000. Neither of these plans was implemented, and a compromise was agreed with the other occupants to allow Oriel more interior space for exhibitions.[25] This arrangement was only a temporary expedient, particularly as far as Oriel 31 was concerned. A public gallery was by now expected, not least by the Arts Council, to have better facilities than required even ten years earlier. In principle, the MCRA backed the remaining extension plan, which was now expected to cost £58,000, but it proved impossible for Oriel to obtain funding.[26]

There is evidence that this led to tension between Oriel 31 and the MCRA. It was suggested in discussions between Oriel 31 and other parties that the MCRA and Powys Rural Council should vacate the Memorial Gallery to allow Oriel full use of the building without the need for an extension.[27] As a result, Montgomery District Council invited the Rural Council to move to its old offices in Llanidloes. The offer was declined, with the full support of the MCRA.[28] The episode revealed to the MCRA, if it was not already aware of it, an attempt to induce it to vacate its one remaining building. It also revealed a fundamental difference in perception. To the MCRA, severing the historic relationship with the Rural Council in this way would be to disregard its own purpose and that of the building. However, from the perspective of the parties that were keen to develop Oriel 31, the MCRA was being intransigent in refusing to vacate a building that should, they believed, be purely a gallery. It was that perception of intransigence that led to, or was used to justify, an entirely different approach to the visual arts in the county.[29]

The Memorial Gallery at Risk: The Mid-Wales Arts Centre

In 1991, Oriel 31 approached the District Council and the Development Board for Rural Wales for match funding for another feasibility study. During that year their aim of obtaining funding for the planned extension of the memorial gallery turned into something much more ambitious. The study that was finally commissioned, with the encouragement of the funding bodies, was for an entirely new and much larger arts centre, to be located in Welshpool.[30] This project, named the Mid Wales Arts Centre, did not involve the MCRA at all, and in the end did not succeed, but as it did have an impact on the plans for Memorial Gallery an outline of its history is necessary.

On the basis of a glowing feasibility study, the Mid Wales Arts Centre Trust obtained the promise of a site in the park of Powis Castle, chosen for its ability to attract visitors from the West Midlands. It had the support of the National Trust, and the promise of significant funding from the Arts Council Lottery Fund. However, it had not secured support or revenue funding from the new unitary authority, Powys County Council, which came into being on 1 April 1996. Without that support, the project could not continue, and it came to an end in October 1996.[31] Until then, it seemed destined to succeed; Arts Council documents referred to the 'impending' arts centre as early as 1993.[32]

The Mid Wales Arts Centre plan created considerable uncertainty about the future of the Davies Memorial Gallery. The immediate impact was to put significant improvements to the building on hold, at a time when the structure was showing its age and was in need of repair. The second problem was that the nature of Oriel's future art provision in the gallery, once the Mid

Wales Arts Centre opened, was unclear. Oriel 31 by now ran a varied programme of exhibitions, many of which it originated; for instance, in 1992-93, while the new arts centre was being planned, eight of the twelve exhibitions at the Memorial Gallery were originated by Oriel 31.[33] However, there was no commitment to continue this, indeed no clear commitment to any exhibition programme at all. Although Oriel requested a new lease, its director, Michael Nixon, declined to give any indication to the MCRA of its future plans, which did nothing to allay the Association's fears for the future of the gallery.[34] The manner of the project's failure also raised questions about the willingness of the new Powys County Council to support gallery provision in the future. The council's attitude would be crucial to any future plans for the Memorial Gallery. That became clearer in 1998 when a county council officer assured the MCRA that it had 'no antipathy' to Oriel 31.[35] Instead, the decision to abandon the Mid-Wales Arts Centre was explained in terms of the council's regional priorities within Powys, in which context the funding required by the project posed a threat to the continued operation of the Newtown gallery.

A New Sense of Purpose: Art and Community

Before the outcome of the Mid Wales Arts Centre plan was known, the MCRA had concluded that action could be postponed no longer, and early in 1996 a working group was put together to look at the future and development of the Memorial Gallery.[36] The group included Islwyn Davies, together with Dr Glyn Tegai Hughes and Chris Tomley, both longstanding members who would continue to play a crucial part in developing the MCRA approach to the Memorial Gallery over the coming years. They concluded that the state of the Memorial Gallery meant that 'it was no longer a fitting memorial to Margaret and Gwendoline Davies'.[37] Because the sisters had been community benefactors, and because Newtown voluntary groups had been unable to fund a purpose-built community centre, the MCRA decided to look into the possibility of incorporating a community centre into the Memorial Gallery.[38] A feasibility study was commissioned from the partnership that had originally designed the building, who recommended demolishing part of the building and constructing new additions.[39] Tensions with Oriel resurfaced, as there were fears that a competing application might damage the Mid-Wales Arts Centre project. The MCRA agreed to wait until the outcome of that was known, not least because it could change the scale of the gallery operation that would be required, but considered it necessary to continue developing its own plans.

There were more feasibility studies. A new consultant was engaged in 1997, funded by the Gwendoline and Margaret Davies Charities and the County Council.[40] PAVO (as the rural council was now named) was the public face of the consultation process.[41] This study convinced the MCRA that because the ageing building needed significant repairs, it should create a new, high quality space rather than patch up parts of the building. The proposal envisaged extending the area that the building covered by constructing a large block to one side to house voluntary groups. The gallery functions would be housed in two new and visually differentiated blocks. These would replace the existing building.

The proposal received a qualified welcome from the town council, which was concerned about increasing the supply of low cost office space when there was already surplus commercial office space in the town.[42] There was more support from the county council, which took the view that Newtown needed a boost following the failure of the previous town development bid. The voluntary sector part of the plan was of particular interest to the county council, as the advantages of shared facilities would help maximize the benefit of the grants they already gave to the organizations concerned. Islwyn Davies was particularly keen to remind the county council that neither it nor the Arts Council had contributed to the original gallery and he was advised to draw attention to the local authority's moral obligation to contribute to a cultural centre following the sale of the Pavilion in 1974.[43]

Despite eighteen months of work on this proposal, and the promise of match funding of £250,000 from the Davies Charities, the resulting application to the Arts

Council for Lottery funds did not succeed. The project was estimated to cost around £2.9 million, and the Arts Council's response was that there would be no funding on that scale available for at least five years (from 1998), if at all. Instead, they suggested that the MCRA should consider alternatives, 'such as releasing the whole building to Oriel 31 or reducing the scale of the bid'.[44] In general terms, the Arts Council appeared more interested in venues concerned purely with the arts than in mixed-use centres. However, it had been aware of, or party to, previous attempts to put pressure on the MCRA to move out of the building, and it is likely that the MCRA was aware of that. The MCRA was, unsurprisingly, determined to resist another attempt by a public body to remove it from the building that had been conceived and paid for by the Davies charities rather than by public funds. After all, it had a history of losing buildings to public bodies with different priorities.

That, however, was not the reasoning it employed with the Arts Council. According to the MCRA's chairman, Glyn Tegai Hughes, the essence of the memorial was the combination of art and community activity. He explained that turning it over solely to Oriel 31 'would not be consonant with the memorial aspect of the building', given that it commemorated two sisters who were not only 'the greatest benefactors of the arts that Wales has ever had, but [whose] charitable support of social causes was of major importance to them'.[45] From this perspective, a memorial to the sisters meant actions rather than simply a name over the door. However, the argument made no noticeable impact on the Arts Council's thinking.

Over the next year, both the MCRA and Oriel 31 went back to the drawing board, and struggled to find a workable strategy. Having to wait five years in the hope the goalposts would have moved in the right direction by then seemed unpromising, while carrying on with the plan to build new voluntary sector rooms (and simply repairing rather than rebuilding the gallery) created new difficulties in getting full funding. The 'fallback' position of repairs and minor improvements would be much cheaper, but it did not solve all the problems of the building, and only part of the repair cost would be eligible for grants. Then there were previously 'unthinkable' possibilities to consider if no extension was possible, such as choosing between devoting the whole building either to the gallery or to the community organizations. As Glyn Tegai Hughes pointed out, both of these possibilities came with problems. Without community rents, how would the gallery meet its running costs? And without the gallery, how would it still be a memorial to the sisters?[46]

Community, Art and Compromise

These questions were not fully resolved by 1999, when the MCRA launched another attempt to get the project off the ground in some form. The MCRA was divided on the way forward, particularly on the question of whether to try splitting the community and cultural aspects of its activities.[47] The discovery that they would have to begin the application process to the Arts Council again from the beginning, requiring another feasibility study and more costs, contributed to an air of exasperation in the internal documents circulated by the Chairman. The new consultants argued that sharing the existing space limited all the occupants in what they could do, but that in practice it was Oriel 31 that came off worst: the voluntary groups were in the wrong building and until they were rehoused the memorial's potential could not be realized. Of the four options they put forward, two involved rehousing the voluntary work somehow. The original plan for a new building was ideal, but a less costly alternative might be to find an existing building for voluntary groups to occupy.[48] There was some disquiet among the MCRA members that the Association's objectives were not fully addressed in all this, that is, the proposals were focused on the needs of the gallery and barely considered the needs of voluntary groups. Moreover, there was no suitable building in sight at the time.

The way forward came from an unexpected direction early in 2000. The MCRA learned that the convent that was then occupying Plas Dolerw intended to move out and sell the building. The MCRA was now ready to consider a compromise. It had exhausted all routes to achieving its ideal solution of combining community activity and the gallery in one building, and in the meantime the voluntary groups were growing desperate for a suitable space. A strong argument was made by David Hall that the MCRA would not be 'playing fair' by those groups if it did not take the opportunity to improve their situation.[49] Plas Dolerw was a good opportunity. It was a fundamentally sound building in an appealing location bordering Dolerw Park, with rooms large enough for events and conferences. The gallery and voluntary activities would be more distant than had been envisaged earlier, as they would be separated by the park, but access to the new site was good. The county council supported the idea, but the parents of children at the neighbouring school first had to be reassured in a public meeting that the safety of their children would be paramount.[50] The MCRA's offer of £195,000 to buy the building was accepted early in 2000 and the following year it took possession of the building.

The purchase of Plas Dolerw was achieved mainly through charitable funding. A sum of £100,000 came from the Gwendoline and Margaret Davies Charity, on condition it would be repaid if the building was sold.[51] Another £40,000 came from the Tudor Trust, and £39,000 was provided by the county council. The rest was funded by cashing in the MCRA's investments. The building needed refurbishment and alterations to house the full range of tenants and events that were envisaged. This work was even more costly than the purchase.

Nonetheless, that still made it half the cost of building a new voluntary sector extension.[52]

This was the start of significant changes to the scale of the MCRA's operations. Since the first working group in 1996, the demands on the building group and in particular the Chairman, Glyn Tegai Hughes, had been enormous. Endless explanatory documents had been needed. The workload increased dramatically in 2000, under the demands of negotiating the purchase, seeking grants and reopening discussions with Oriel and the consultants about revising plans for the Memorial Gallery. In September of that year, Glyn Tegai Hughes reported that the small project group had been meeting three times per week to deal with these matters. The group at that stage included Islwyn Davies, Chris Tomley and Peter English, as well as Dr Hughes, who were crucial to the success of the project.

The immediate need was for more help to undertake significant fundraising, and the building needed a manager before it could generate an income. The MCRA obtained revenue grants from the Davies Charities to supplement its small income, which allowed Angela Williams to move from PAVO to the MCRA to fill these roles, and the team was assisted for several weeks by Robyn Hill, through a 'Growth Graduate' scheme. The fundraising efforts succeeded in raising another £230,000 for the refurbishment, most of it from the Community Fund. The MCRA's new community sector tenants, together with PAVO, moved into Plas Dolerw in the spring of 2002.

Oriel Davies Gallery

The consultants to the Memorial Gallery project were delighted: the gallery aspect of the project had been transformed. The existing gallery would be available to Oriel 31 in its entirety, which would give more security both to them and to their funders, the Arts Council. Oriel 31 would be on a level playing field with the other ten revenue-funded galleries in Wales, and it would be able to display work on loan from the National Gallery of Wales and other major galleries. Education and community programmes and exhibitions would benefit from expanded facilities too. The consultants concluded that the project was now much clearer and a much better proposition for capital and revenue funding from a wide range of sources, not least because the gallery would 'be able to make a greater cultural, social and educational contribution to the region'.[53]

It was still not certain that funding for an extension to the gallery could be achieved, but the consultants were clear that even without one the Memorial Gallery would be a vast improvement once reconfigured. They listed the elements essential for the building to function well as a gallery, which could be achieved without an extension. It needed a new roof, office space for the gallery staff and storage space. And they were adamant that Oriel should have sole use of both galleries. It would also be desirable to replace the existing dismal meeting room with a larger room refurbished for educational use. But with even a small extension it could achieve this more comfortably and add space for a small shop and coffee bar too. Good coffee bars and shops were not luxuries, they advised, but added considerably to the attractions in galleries or museums. If professionally run, they would draw people in, encourage them to linger and provide a modest income.

But not all principles were agreed. The Arts Council required Oriel 31 to have complete autonomy to run its own affairs, which was not disputed. The MCRA wanted to retain symbolic use of an office in the building, while the consultants and Oriel 31 interpreted autonomy to mean exclusive control of the entire building. Retention of office space in this way was rejected precisely because of what it symbolized. The already tense relationship between Oriel 31 and the MCRA broke down badly in 2000, when the attitude of Oriel representatives in negotiations about terms of occupancy caused great offence to the MCRA members present. This was sufficiently serious for a new negotiating team to be required.[54] Relationships must have been repaired somehow, however, as negotiations eventually concluded, although the terms were in the end largely dictated by the Arts Council.

Both the MCRA and Oriel realized that divisions had to be overcome, and during the course of the project development each invited observers from the other body to sit on their management councils. Even with the assistance of consultants, architects and project managers, the gallery project would become more demanding and the workload more intense. The MCRA had taken on an even more complex project, on a scale more often seen in fully-staffed organizations than in voluntary groups. It demanded both creativity and long hours by members of the volunteer project group. It also brought new financial risks for the MCRA. The planned expenditure was over £1 million, and the MCRA could not afford to meet any unscheduled costs. The gallery project could not be successfully achieved without stringent financial control, and David Hall took on that role as the new Treasurer. The MCRA had assumed greater responsibilities, and with them the need for vigilant governance.

By the time the MCRA moved into Plas Dolerw in 2002 it was ready to go ahead with the first of three phases in the redevelopment of the Memorial Gallery. Grant funding had been lined up from the Arts Council, the Gwendoline and Margaret Davies charities, the County Council and other sources, and fundraising was under way for the remaining two phases.[55] In the first phase a small extension was achieved without the need for additional land, meaning it was not necessary to renegotiate the terms of its very cheap lease. It created a coffee bar on the north side of the building, which brought more light and liveliness into the building as well as space. The main exhibition space was at last refurbished to contemporary standards. To achieve this, the Memorial Gallery was closed for the rest of the year and the gallery staff were temporarily relocated to Plas Dolerw.

Work on the next two phases started in 2004. This restructured the two outer blocks of the building, while the gallery operations resumed in the central portion.[56] The work created a second permanent exhibition space from the old conference room. At the same time the foyer was expanded and a shop was created by removing a cluttered arrangement of offices and stores, as well as an education room and resource area. The result was an uncluttered and flexible gallery arrangement and an attractive and sociable foyer and café, at a total cost of just under £1.5 million. It was a matter of some pride that the Treasurer's efforts were rewarded by completing it under budget, apparently a novel experience for the Arts Council. The newly refurbished building was officially opened by Lembit Opik MP at the end of January 2005.[57] By then, both the building and the gallery operation (formerly Oriel 31) had been re-named Oriel Davies Gallery.

CONCLUSIONS

It has been an eventful hundred years for the MCRA. In part, that is the inevitable trajectory of a story beginning in 1919 in the wake of one devastating world war and continuing through the second in 1939-45 and beyond. But the events dealt with here are those that the MCRA created or influenced.

The MCRA began in a blaze of glory, its creation being reported by the press across Britain. Within the county it aroused widespread enthusiasm for action, for participation in sporting and cultural activities, and simply for raising the prospect of a more cheerful life. Dozens of people participated in the numerous committees that dreamed up sports day events, set up new clubs and planned with great thoroughness the musical education of the county, while hundreds more participated directly in sports teams and the rapidly growing number of choirs. The memory of these achievements dissipated over time, but two others were more enduring: the network of village institutes and the County Music Festival. Both of these initiatives left a visible legacy, and the music festival became increasingly important to the MCRA's identity.

The MCRA was among the pioneers of a new approach to voluntary work. It was at first centralized, and even autocratic, in the way it operated but later it developed a more collaborative approach that better suited the way in which its work had changed. Its early achievements now needed nurturing, and new activities called for quiet support and occasional advocacy. It prefigured the new rural community councils that were set up across the rest of Wales in the 1930s, but whereas most of them were under pressure to adopt the same model as that already in use in England, the attempt to do the same in Montgomeryshire ended with a compromise. Those involved in the MCRA did set up a county rural community council, which may have been no more than a committee of the MCRA, but before the end of the 1930s that had fully merged into the MCRA. From then until 1975, the identities of the MCRA and the notional rural community council merged to the point of being indistinguishable, even to those involved with them, and the memory of their origins became blurred. But then the MCRA had to rediscover its origins, its identity and its purpose, as it was forced to disentangle its work from that of the newly independent rural council. It was a reluctant divorce, and it took a long time to discover a new identity.

However, at the end of the twentieth century the MCRA found a new sense of purpose, and in the first five years of the new century this led it to invest close to £1.9 million in both arts and community provision. Oriel Davies was an achievement a long time in the making, not least because the MCRA was unwilling to sacrifice its ideals of supporting community action in order to achieve it. It took ten years from the MCRA's first plan for an integrated arts and community building to achieve the highly regarded, medium-scale gallery that Oriel Davies became in 2005. It was more than fifteen years since Oriel had first suggested an extension. And it was almost forty years since the gallery's beginnings. The new sense of purpose that the MCRA discovered at the beginning of the twenty-first century turned the building into the kind of memorial to the Davies sisters that it seemed to promise when it was built in 1967. Equally importantly, it led the MCRA to increase its commitment to community action, rather than to reduce it, with the establishment of Plas Dolerw as a voluntary sector centre.

After losing both its parallel existence as a Community Council and its community sector premises in the 1970s, the MCRA had adapted to its new reduced circumstances. In doing so it became a small voluntary organization that happened to own a gallery building. Those circumstances had been forced on it by other bodies and policies, and it seemed for some years that it would continue to be buffeted by similar forces beyond its control. That changed decisively when it decided to take control of the development of the gallery building, although it did not always feel like that to those involved. It is clear that its trustees in this period were both highly motivated and very able, and between them they displayed the drive and tenacity that characterized the major investments of the MCRA's early years. But, crucially, they did so with none of the financial crises that occurred in the earlier period. This time round the achievements were secured through flexibility. There was a willingness to compromise on the *means* by which the MCRA's aims could be achieved, rather than on the *aims* themselves.

The exemplary management of the project costs also earned the MCRA new respect among the bodies it dealt with. This respect may have contributed to its successful intervention in the campaign to save Newtown Textile Museum. This former weaving factory had been purchased by volunteers in 1964 and set up as a charitable museum trust. After struggling financially, it was transferred to Powys County Council in 1990 and the charity was closed down in 2003. When the council decided to close the museum and sell the building in 2015, local volunteers mounted a campaign to save it. The MCRA was able to assist by persuading the county council to hand it the property by way of a Community Asset Transfer. It is unlikely that would have succeeded had the MCRA not already shown itself capable of managing complex projects. The museum reopened in 2016 under the MCRA's stewardship and operated by volunteers. The aim is that eventually the volunteers will be able to form an independent charity to manage the museum.[1] In that way, the MCRA will be able to resume its preferred role of supporting other voluntary groups by ensuring they have the premises they need.

APPENDICES

Appendix I: Extract from the 'Rules of the Association'

The source for this extract is an undated booklet, which is almost certainly the printed rule book that was adopted at the first annual meeting in July 1920. There are no later references to such a booklet. It can be dated to between 1920 and 1926, as follows. Rule 13(c) – not reproduced below – names the first trustees, who were not appointed until 1920, while other rules were changed in 1926.

The extract reproduces rules 3 and 4.

3. Objects

The objects of the Association are recreation in its widest and most liberal sense, and to this end to establish and carry on social, recreative and educational work and institutions; to provide village halls, institutions, and public recreation grounds where such do not exist, and to promote the moral, mental, and physical training and culture of the inhabitants of the county of Montgomery and the adjoining counties; to improve the condition of the working and poorer classes and provide them with the means of healthy recreation in their leisure time; to co-operate with the Educational Authorities in the different localities in promoting primary and secondary education and to assist in the provision of playing fields where such do not exist, and generally to further and assist in such other educational, social and charitable objects as in the opinion of the Association may promote the welfare of the inhabitants of the said county, and without limitation of the foregoing to carry out the following work, that is to say:-

(a) To revive, originate, organise and develop all forms of recreative activities within the area of the Association.
(b) To form in each locality a Local Recreation Association, responsible for all recreative activities in that locality.
(c) To assist local efforts in obtaining suitable grounds and institutes.
(d) To stimulate the development of local recreation by:
    1. Organising County and League events, and circuits of of matches, etc., in the various districts.
    2. Arranging concerts, lectures, debates, eisteddfodau, festivals, etc.
    3. Arranging for a professional or professionals, whose services will be at the disposal of local clubs.
    4. Providing trophies and prizes.
    5. Entering into contracts for recreative requisites in bulk and selling to clubs at reduced prices.
    6. Circulating literature and films.
    7. Securing lecturers, adjudicators, artistes, etc.
    8. Arranging for columns in the local press.
    9. Paying attention to the organisation of recreation for schools and the development of physical culture.
(e) To co-ordinate its efforts with those of the Local Authorities, Comrades of the Great War, Women's Institutes, and other organisations.
(f) To introduce new and improved forms of recreative activity into the area of the Association.

(g) To avoid overlapping caused by the increasing number of county organisations which are all working in a recreative direction.
(h) To keep the standard and the tone of all forms of recreation as high as possible.
(i) To start a county organisation that will serve as a model and be of use to other counties.
(j) To provide for all other organisations outside the county, that may have facilities to offer, a county completely organised and ready to receive and use facilities in the fullest and most profitable manner.

4. Scope

The following activities shall come within the purview of the Association:-

Outdoor Recreation	*Indoor Recreation*
Football	Concerts
Hockey	Lectures
Cricket	Badminton
Tennis	Cinemas
Bowling	Eisteddfodau
Hunting	Music Societies
Croquet	Music Festivals
Golf	Dramatic Societies
Quoits	Debating Societies
Athletic Sports	Bands
Cycling	Boxing
Field Clubs	Chess
Angling	Billiards
Physical Training	Draughts
Swimming	Dancing
Boy Scouts	Whist Drives
Girl Guides	Miniature Rifle Shooting

and any others that the Executive Committee may adopt.

Appendix II: The Davies family financial contribution

Special donations and capital funding 1919-50

These are funds donated to establish and secure the MCRA. The available sources do not always specify the individual donor or the purpose of the donation. Donations in the first two years cannot be traced with a great deal of certainty, owing to the fragmentary nature of accounting records for the first two years, consequently these have been estimated from newspaper reports. The resulting estimates correspond sufficiently with reserves reported in 1922 to give a reasonable baseline for the funding that established the MCRA. However, it is possible that some donations have been omitted, hence the tables below estimate the minimum capital donations made by the Davies family to the MCRA.

Donations by Year

Year	Purpose	David Davies £	Gwendoline & Margaret Davies £	Davies family (unattrib.) £
1919-20	Trophies & shields, estimate	50		
	Llandinam ground (8) (10)	400		
	Caersws ground (8) (10)	450 (a)		
1920-21	Cinema Lory (2)	925		
	County Ground (2)	2,400		
	Newtown Football Ground (2)	475		
	Special Donations (1)			8,000 (b)
1921-22	Special Donations (11)			11,258 (b)
1922-23	Welshpool Recreation Ground (3) (10)	1,340		
	Other Special Donations (3)	4,244		
1923-24	Special Donations (3) (10)	682		
1924-25	Pavilion fixtures (3)		122	
	Machynlleth Recreation Ground (3)	450		
	Sarn Recreation Ground (3)	175		
1925-26	Donations, reconfiguration (3)	3,000	5,450	
subtotal	*Special Donations*	*13,909*	*5,572*	*19,258*

		£	£	£
1920-21	Loan, Cinema equipment (4)	1,824		
1921-22	Loan, unspecified (3)	1,000		
	Loan, Pavilion (3)		2,000	
1924-25	Loan, Pavilion fixtures (3)		123	
1934-35	Mortgage, Severn Place (3)		1,800	
1941-42	Mortgage, Pavilion (3)		1,000	
	Less net repayments	(125)		
subtotal	*Loans and Mortgages cancelled in 1944 (5)*	*2,699*	*4,923*	*19,258*
Total	**Special donations & gifts**	**16,608**	**10,495**	**19,258**

Donations by Purpose

	David Davies £	Gwendoline & Margaret Davies £	Davies family (unattrib.) £
	£	£	£
Gifts in kind: grounds, trophies, lorry	6,665		
Specified purposes: Pavilion, Cinema, Severn Place	2,699	5,045	
Unspecified. Includes funding Institutes (9)	4,244		19,258
Bail-out funding 1926 (3)	3,000	5,450	
	16,608	**10,495**	**19,258**

The equivalent value in 2018 of these capital donations, estimated on the basis of the retail price index (rpi) is approximately £2.3 million.

Notes

(a) Grounds donated directly to local associations do not appear here as they will not appear in the MCRA financial records. For instance, early minutes and reports refer to David Davies's promise to donate a site in Tregynon which does not appear in the records: it is likely that the donation was to the Tregynon local association.

(b) No accounts or financial records exist for this period; the only sources are the *Express* reports of the 1920 and 1921 annual meetings. As the *Express* reports of subsequent meetings are consistent with the MCRA records, it has been assumed that the amounts reported on these occasions are also accurate.

(c) Present values shown for comparative purposes indicate the scale of magnitude only. Retail price index (rpi) is an unreliable measure over long time periods or when comparing periods of very different economic structure, both of which apply here. The Bank of England historic rpi calculator was used. An alternative approach to assessing the value of these sums is to compare with contemporary salaries: the Music Organizer was paid £450 p.a. in 1921-25, while from 1925 the secretary's salary was £300 p.a.

Revenue funding, 1926-50. As well as the capital sums above, David, Gwendoline and Margaret Davies each made donations towards the general running costs of the

Association. According to contemporary press reports donations in the first year amounted to £1,425 of which £600 came from the Misses Davies and £673 from their brother (6). Donations in the second year (to March 1921) were noted in a press report which expressed disappointment that so few had contributed to the Association: of the £654 donated, £600 came from the Misses Davies (7).

MCRA records do not give any indication of the financial value of the secondment of the first secretary, Captain J. Glynn Jones, during the first two years, which would represent a donation in kind by David Davies. In 1922, David Davies donated £300, after which his donations were categorized as special donations (listed above). In the same year his sisters gave £50 each to the general funds and most or all of the £515 donated to the music festival.

After that, Gwendoline and Margaret made donations each year until 1950, of amounts ranging from £330 to £550, initially to the music festival and later (after 1926) to the Association's central funds. Until the end of the war, their contributions were sufficient to pay the organizer's salary, so continued to provide crucial support for the Festival; afterwards, as salaries increased, the proportion of running costs covered by their donation rapidly declined. Other support in kind, such as hosting music festival conferences at Gregynog, is not captured by financial analysis.

Davies Charities' Funding, 1950-2018

Revenue funding, 1950–2018. There was a hiatus in 1951, the year Gwendoline Davies died. In 1952, annual payments to the MCRA resumed at a rate of £300 per year until 1972, now recorded as coming from the sisters' charities. There is no evidence that this payment continued beyond this date. Other revenue grants may have been paid sporadically but they have not been traced. Between 2001 and 2018, revenue grants from the Davies sisters' charity were made each year, with the exception of 2002. The sums varied between £2,000 and £10,000 per year, and amounted to £73,873 in total.

Capital donations 1950–2018

		£
1967	Donation of the Davies Memorial Gallery (d)	£39,400
2001-5	Grant towards purchase of Plas Dolerw (e)	£100,000
2001-5	Grant for Davies Memorial Gallery extension and refurbishment (e)	£250,000
	Total	**£389,400**

The equivalent value in 2018, estimated on the basis of rpi, is approximately £1.24 million.

Notes

(d) The Davies Memorial Gallery cost £45,227 (the historic cost before depreciation, as stated in the Association's financial statements for 1994 and later). Entries in the

Margaret Davies Charity accounts show that between 1966 and 1969 donations of £39,400 were made to the MCRA (at the 2019 value this is approximately £700,000). It is reasonable to assume that these donations funded the construction of the gallery. The source of the remaining £5,827 has not been identified.

(e) These grants were given as match funding, which allowed the MCRA to raise additional grants for the two projects. The Association's financial statements indicate that total funding for the two projects amounted to £1,976,501.

Sources: (1) *Express*, 7 December 1920; (2) MCRA, Secretary's Report, 30 November 1920; (3) MCRA, Annual Accounts for the year or later years; (4) MCRA, Cinema ledger; (5) MCRA, Annual General Meeting, 2 February 1945; (6) *County Times*, 10 July 1920; (7) *Express*, 29 March 1921; (8) MCRA, Secretary's Report, 13 December 1919; (9) MCRA, Accounts for 1925; (10) MCRA, Journal (ledger), 1922; (11) *Express*, 11 October 1921.

Appendix III: Village Institutes erected by the MCRA

MCRA minutes suggest that twenty institutes were completed by February 1922, and two were begun after that date. Of those, only seventeen are supported by strong evidence; for the remainder, evidence of intention or commencement has been found, but not evidence of completion. One, at Bishops Castle, seems unlikely, since it had earlier been denied membership of the MCRA.

Institute	***Date of opening***		***Sources***
Abermule	11 November 1920		**(a)**
Arddleen	23 October 1921		**(a) (c)**
Banwy Valley/Garthbeibio	Not recorded		**(c) (f)**
Bettws	16 December 1921		**(a) (c)**
Bishops Castle	Not recorded		(e)
Bwlchyffridd	8 December 1921		**(a) (c)**
Caersws	December 1920		**(a) (b)**
Carno	Not recorded	To be paid for by MCRA	(d)
Chirbury	27 December 1921		**(a) (c)**
Churchstoke	6 January 1922		**(a) (c)**
Guilsfield	Not recorded		**(c)** (f)
Hyssington	16 November 1921		**(a) (c)**
Llanbrynmair	25 December 1920		**(a) (b) (c)**

Llandrinio	10 November 1921		**(a) (c)**
Llanfechain	Not recorded		(e)
Meifod	3 February 1922		**(a)** (e)
New Mills	26 December 1920		**(b) (c)**
Penybontfawr	10 January 1922		**(a)**
Sarn	Not recorded		(g)
Tregynon	18 January 1922	Paid for by MCRA	**(a) (c)**
Van	17 November 1921		**(a) (c)**

Minutes have been supplemented by accounting records and press reports. Nonetheless, not all MCRA institutes can be identified with equal certainty. Sources a-c (shown above in bold type) provide the strongest evidence. The institutes that were paid for in full by the MCRA appear to have been transferred to the ownership of the local association.

Sources

(a) Date of opening recorded in minutes (executive committee) 11 February 1922.

(b) Date of opening and MCRA funding reported in the *Express.*

(c) Confirmed by examining accounting records of construction debt reduced or written off.

(d) Minutes record the intention to erect this at no cost to the local Association, there is only partial evidence of related costs in accounting records. This may have been the village hall that was destroyed by fire in 1938.

(e) Minutes (executive committee) record as in progress, 30 November 1920 or March 1921.

(f) Minutes (executive committee) record acceptance of tenders, 11 February 1922.

(g) In progress according to *Express* 18 October 1921, reporting 1921 annual meeting.

Appendix IV: People – Presidents, Officers and Others

Patron

David Davies, MP; later 1st Baron Davies	1919-44

Presidents

David Davies, MP, later 1st Baron Davies	1919-44
Margaret S. Davies	1945-49
Hon. Islwyn E. E. Davies	1949- 64
Col. E. C. Powell	1964-73
D. Bret Jehu	1973-86
Hon. Jonathon Davies	1986-2001
David Davies, 3rd Baron Davies	2002-present

Secretaries and Organizers

Capt. John Glynn Jones, MC	Secretary and organizer; seconded from David Davies' staff, full-time until 1921. A less frequent presence in 1921-23, when he worked with boys clubs in south Wales.	1919-23
Oliver D. S. Taylor	Assistant secretary Remained a member of MCRA Music and Finance committees into the 1930s.	1920–25

J. M. Nicholas	Music organizer	1920-24
J. E. Tomley	Secretary for re-organization period. He had been a member of the executive committee since 1921, representing Montgomery, and a member of the short-lived summer sports committee.	1923-26
Edward Jones	Secretary Previously secretary of the North Wales Village Clubs Association	1925-48
Hywel Davies	Rural Industries Organizer	1946-68
Gwilym Havard Rees	Secretary	1948-65
Edgar Spooner	Secretary Previously secretary to the Radnor Rural Community Council, among other posts. Became first secretary of the Powys Rural Community Council in 1975.	1965-75

The MCRA did not employ a secretary or equivalent officer in this period. Company Secretary and administrative services were provided under an agency agreement with Powys Rural Council (PRC) / PAVO. The following acted as Company Secretary:	1975-2000

Edgar Spooner (PRC) 1975-81

Peter Dean (PRC) 1981–97

Angela Williams (PAVO) 1997-2000

Angela Williams	Company secretary and manager	2001-12
Clair J. Stevens	Company secretary and manager	2012 – present

Trustees 1919- 1950

It is unlikely that this list is complete, as more than one trustee was needed at any time.

Edward Jones	Maesmawr Hall, Caersws	1920-37
A. E. Humphreys Owen	Glansevern, Berriew	1920-30
Capt. J. Murray Naylor	Leighton Hall, Welshpool	1920-31
Mr Evan Emrys Jones	Maesmawr Hall, Caersws	1930-48

Col. George R. D. Harrison	Welshpool Also a member from 1919, Chairman for many years in the 1930s-40s, and mayor of Welshpool in the 1930s. He also encouraged the formation of rural community councils.	1930-50

Selected members

The Association had many members and officers during its hundred year history. Those listed here are limited to people named in the text but not listed above, who played a significant role in the two major building periods: 1919-26 and 1990-2006.

1919-1926

Major W. J. Burdon-Evans	The dominant practical influence in the Associations first thirty years, as the first chairman, 1919-29, and executive and finance committee member until shortly before his death in 1949. He was David Davies' private business secretary until 1931, then adviser to the Davies sisters at Gregynog. He was involved in many other voluntary causes in the county.
Miss Gwendoline E. Davies	Vice-President; supporter and donor until her death in 1951.

J. T. C. Gittins	Member and legal adviser from 1919 until his death in 1959.
W. H. Leslie	Member of the music and eisteddfod committee since its inception. He was its Chairman in 1921, and presided over the evening session of the first County Music Festival.
W. E. Pryce-Jones	Vice-President in 1922, served on sports and finance committees, member and supporter from 1919 until his death in 1949.
1990 - 2006	
Islwyn E. E Davies	After his period as President, he remained a member of the MCRA council until his death in 2002. He was a member of the project groups that dealt with successive proposals for the Memorial Gallery, and provided vigorous support for the MCRA throughout. It was his idea to present the Memorial Gallery to the MCRA. In tribute the MCRA agreed that Oriel Davies and Plas Dolerw would not have come to fruition without his support. (MCRA, AGM, 2002)
Peter English	Member 1999 – 2010, Treasurer 2005-2010. He was a member of the project groups that dealt with successive proposals for the Memorial Gallery, to which he brought the perspective of his profession of Chartered Surveyor.

David Hall	Member of the MCRA from 1997 to the present, Treasurer 2001-2005, Chairman 2005 to the present. Another key member during the refurbishment of the Memorial Gallery and purchase of Plas Dolerw, and responsible for its exemplary cost control. Former local government officer, with special interest in community development.
Dr Glyn Tegai Hughes	Member of the MCRA from 1988 – 2017, Chairman from 1997 – 2005, in which role he led the refurbishment of the Memorial Gallery and purchase of Plas Dolerw. Vice-President 2005-2017. Former academic and Warden of Gregynog, and brought a profound understanding of the aims and ethos that underpinned the projects that the Davies sisters supported at Gregynog and in Montgomeryshire.
Christopher Tomley	Member of the MCRA from 1986 – 2002 and 2014 to the present, Vice President 1999-2002. He was an active member of the project groups that dealt with successive proposals for the Memorial Gallery, and as a solicitor offered a great deal of *pro bono* legal advice.

NOTES

1

[1] Revd Gwilym Davies, 'Wales at Work: A Social Diary', *Welsh Outlook; a monthly journal of national social progress*, Vol. 7, No. 4 (1 April 1920), p. 101.

[2] *Montgomery County Times* (henceforth *County Times*), 26 July 1919.

[3] *Montgomeryshire Express and Radnor Times* (henceforth *Express*), 22 July 1919.

[4] *County Times*, 27 July 1919.

[5] *County Times*, 26 July 1919.

[6] *Express*, 29 July 1919.

[7] *Express*, 29 July 1919.

[8] *Express*, 29 July 1919.

[9] *Express*, 22 July 1919.

[10] *Express*, 29 July 1919.

[11] MCRA, *Pamphlet 3: Rules of the Association* (undated). See Appendix I.

[12] Rule 3, *ibid.*

[13] MCRA, Annual Report, 1958-9. The Chairman referred to was Major Burden-Owen, who was employed by David Davies as his Business Secretary.

[14] *Llandinam*, 3 (June 1901). Web, llandinam-lives.org.uk. Accessed 4 April 2919.

[15] *Llandinam*, 3 (June 1901).

[16] Robert Snape, Leisure, *Voluntary Action and Social Change in Britain, 1880-1939* (New York, 2018).

[17] MCRA, Minutes and Secretary's Report, 16 March 1920.

[18] MCRA, Minutes, Executive Committee 16 September 1919.

2

[1] MCRA, Minutes of the Executive Committee, 16 March 1920.

[2] MCRA, Minutes of the Executive Committee, 6 July 1920.

[3] Report on the MCRA's March Executive meeting, *Express*, 29 March 1921.

[4] MCRA, Secretary's Report, Executive Committee, 30 November 1920.

[5] MCRA, Minutes of the Executive Committee, 16 September 1919.

[6] MCRA, Minutes of the Executive Committee, 9 March 1920.

[7]Bank of England calculator, 1920:2018. www.bankofengland.co.uk. Accessed 30 April 2019. The bank warns that retail price comparisons across such a long period of time are inherently unreliable.
[8] MCRA, Minutes of the Executive Committee, 30 November 1920.
[9] *Express*, 1 February 1921.
[10] MCRA, Minutes of the Summer Sports Sub-committee, 30 March 1920, 6 May 1920.
[11] *County Times*, 2 October 1920.
[12] MCRA, Minutes of the Executive committee, 13 December 1919.
[13] MCRA, Minutes of the Executive Committee, 6 July 1920, appendix 11.
[14] *Express*, 29 March 1921. Report of the MCRA Executive Committee meeting in March 1921.
[15] These were the Amateur Athletic Association and the National Cyclists' Union.
[16] MCRA, Minutes of the County Sports committee, 7 May 1920, 10 May 1920; Summer Sports sub-committee, 11 June 1920.
[17] *Express*, 17 August 1920.
[18] *Express*, 27 July 1920.
[19] *County Times*, 31 July 1920.
[20] MCRA, Minutes of the Sports Committee, 18 May 1920.
[21] *County Times*, 31 July 1920.
[22] *Express*, 7 December 1920. Report on the meeting of the MCRA Executive Committee. The report ran to seven columns.
[23] MCRA, Secretary's report, 26 March 1921.
[24] *County Times*, 1 July 1922.
[25] David Pugh, 'How the County Pavilion Came to Newtown', *The Newtonian* Vol. 15, Autumn 2003.
[26] MCRA, *Annual Report* for 1921-2, p. 8.
[27] MCRA, Accounts for 1923-4.

3

[1] Harold Lacey, 'The Village Clubs Association', *The Town Planning Review* (1921), pp. 166-8; (166).
[2] *County Times,* 13 November 1920. For example: Lord Shaftesbury (who wanted to regain 'Merrie England'), Lord Bleddisloe (who believed there were too many C3 men in rural areas), and Lord Lee, Minister of Agriculture.
[3] Lacey, 'The Village Clubs Association', pp. 166-7; MCRA, Secretary's report, 1926.
[4] MCRA, Minutes, Secretary's report, 1920 (undated).

[5] MCRA, Minutes, Secretary's report, 6 July 1920.
[6] MCRA, Pamphlet no. 1, 8 August 1919.
[7] *Express*, 13 July 1920.
[8] MCRA, Minutes of the Executive committee, 10 February 1920.
[9] MCRA, Minutes, Secretary's report, 1920 (undated).
[10] *Express*, 18 October 1921.
[11] MCRA, Minutes, Secretary's report, 30 November 1920.
[12] *Express*, 10 May 1921.
[13] MCRA, Minutes, Secretary's report, 30 November 1920.
[14] *Express*, 11 October 1921.
[15] MCRA, Minutes of the Executive Committee, 10 February 1920.
[16] MCRA, Journal (Ledger) 1921-1946, p. 26.
[17] *Express*, 29 March 1921, report on MCRA Executive Committee meeting.
[18] MCRA, Minutes of the Village Institute sub-committee, 3 March 1920.
[19] MCRA, Minutes of the Village institute sub-committee, 4 June 1920.
[20] MCRA, Minutes of the Executive committee, 11 February 1922. See Appendix III.
[21] *County Times*, 20 November1920.
[22] *Express*, 7 December 1920.
[23] *Express*, 28 December 1920.
[24] *Express*, 11 January 1921.
[25] *Express*, 7 December 1920.
[26] MCRA, Minutes of the Annual meeting, 6 July 1920.
[27] MCRA, Minutes, Secretary's report, 16 March 1920.
[28] *County Times*, 27 November1920.
[29] *Express*, 29 March 1921, report on MCRA Executive Committee meeting.
[30] Composite figure reconstructed from: MCRA Annual Accounts 1925 and 1924; Journal (ledger) 1921-46, p. 10.
[31] MCRA, Minutes of the Executive committee, 11 February 1922.
[32] See Appendix II.
[33] MCRA, Minutes of the Executive committee, 6 June 1920.
[34] H. Noel Jerman, 'The effects of the winds of change', *The Montgomeryshire Society* (1978).
[35] *Express*, 11 October 1921.
[36] *Express*, 11 October 1921. See Appendix II.
[37] *Hansard*, House of Commons Debates, 27 May 1924, Vol. 174, column 215.
[38] Lacey, 'The Village Clubs Association', p. 167.
[39] MCRA, Minutes of the Executive committee, 10 February 1920.
[40] MCRA, Minutes, 1919-1920; Appendix 11.
[41] MCRA, Minutes, 1919-1920; Appendix 11.
[42] MCRA, Minutes of the Executive committee, 6 July 1920.
[43] MCRA, Minutes of the Executive committee, 30 November 1920.
[44] *County Times*, 27 November 1920.
[45] MCRA, Annual Report, 1922, p. 7.

[46] MCRA, Minutes of the Music festival committee, 24 September 1921.
[47] MCRA, Minutes of the Music festival committee, 24 September 1921.
[48] *Express*, 19 July 1921.
[49] *Express*, 26 July 1921.
[50] *Express*, 26 July 1921.
[51] *Express*, 9 August 1921.
[52] MCRA, Conveyance, 1925.
[53] MCRA, Minutes of the Music and Eisteddfod Committee, 28 September 1922.
[54] MCRA, Minutes of the Music and Eisteddfod Committee, 10 February 1923.
[55] MCRA, Organizers' report, Music and Eisteddfod Committee, 17 March 1923.
[56] *Express*, 1 February 1921.
[57] *Express*, 23 November 1920.
[58] 'Owain Ddu' in the *Express*, 22 June 1920
[1] MCRA, Journal (ledger), 1921-46, pp. 10-48.
[2] MCRA, Annual Report, 1922.
[3] Calculation obtained from the Bank of England calculator, 1921:2018. www.bankofengland.co.uk. Accessed 30 May 2019. The Bank warns that retail price comparisons across such a long period of time are inherently unreliable.
[4] MCRA, Minutes of the Special Executive Committee, 31 May 1924.
[5] MCRA, Accounts, 1926.
[6] Detailed in Appendix II.
[7] MCRA, Minutes of the Music and Eisteddfod Committee, 14 July 1934; 5 December 1936; 10 July 1937.
[8] MCRA, Minutes of the Music and Eisteddfod Committee, 4 December 1933.
[9] John Hywel, 'Music during the Davies period', in Glyn Tegai Hughes, Prys Morgan and G. T. Thomas, *Gregynog* (Cardiff, 1977).
[10] MCRA, Minutes of the Music and Eisteddfod Committee, 9 September 1937.
[11] *Western Daily Press,* 18 July 1935 refers to the 7th annual Children's Music Festival. There was at least one children's music festival held prior to 1925 at Gregynog.
[12] MCRA, Minutes of the Annual General Meeting, 1926.
[13] MCRA, Minutes of the Special Executive Committee, 3 May 1924.
[14] MCRA, Accounts, 1926.
[15] MCRA, Minutes of the Council, 24 August 1932.
[16] MCRA, Secretary's Report, November 1926.
[17] *Express*, 25 February 1939.
[18] MCRA, Minutes of the Annual General Meeting, 1938. The Welsh organizer of the National Fitness Council in 1938 was Captain J. Glynn Jones.
[19] MCRA, Minutes of the Executive Committee report, 6 October1928.

[20] MCRA, Minutes of the Annual General Meeting, 8 November 1930.
[21] MCRA, Minutes of the Music and Eisteddfod Committee, 9 September 1937.
[22] MCRA, Minutes of the Special Council, 24 August 1932.
[23] MCRA, Minutes of the Council, 28 March 1934; Finance and General Purposes Committee, 5 January 1934.
[24] The relevant asset values in 1928 were £4,561 and in 1938 £1,105. The reduction was a result of sales of grounds.
[25] MCRA, Minutes of the Council, 20 February 1931.
[26] www.fieldsintrust.org/history. Accessed 17 May 2019.
[27] MCRA, Minutes of the Council, 28 March 1934.
[28] *Western Mail*, 5 November 1927.
[29] MCRA, Minutes of the Finance and General Purposes Committee, 1 March 1931.
[30] MCRA, Minutes of the Finance and General Purposes Committee, 28 October 1932.
[31] *Express*, 14 February 1933.
[32] MCRA, Minutes of the Finance and General Purposes Committee, 18 September 1937.
[33] MCRA, Minutes of the Finance and General Purposes Committee, 24 September 1932
[34] *Express*, 28 March 1933.
[35] *Express*, 2 May 1933.
[36] *Express,* 19 September 1933.
[37] MCRA, Minutes of the Finance and General Purposes Committee, 16 October 1931.
[38] MCRA, Minutes of the Council, 8 November 1930.
[39] E. L. Ellis, *T.J.: A Life of Dr Thomas Jones, C.H.* (Cardiff, 1992), p. 340.

5

[1] MCRA, minutes of the Music and Eisteddfod Committee, 16 September 1939.
[2] MCRA, minutes of the Music and Eisteddfod Committee, 27 September 1940.
[3] MCRA, correspondence (files a-c), letter from D. Rogers-Hughes, 25 January 1945.
[4] MCRA, correspondence (files a-c), letter from Edward Jones, 29 January 1945.
[5] MCRA, correspondence (files a-c), letter from A. L. Latham, 8 December 1947.
[6] MCRA, minutes of Annual General Meeting, 2 February 1945.
[7] E. L. Ellis, *T.J.: A Life of Dr Thomas Jones, C.H.* (Cardiff, 1992), p. 508.
[8] *Express*, 22 January 1949.
[9] H. Noel Jerman, 'The effects of the winds of change', *The Montgomeryshire Society* (1978).
[10] MCRA, Annual Accounts 1954, for example.
[11] MCRA, Annual Report 1952. The claim may have been inaccurate. The North Powys Music Festival held in 1924 at Bryntanat, the home of Mr W H Leslie, advertised the presence of the Liverpool Philharmonic Orchestra. *County Times* 26 June 1924.
[12] MCRA, Montgomery County Music Committee, 1960-70, Constitution. The new association envisaged that in practice the MCRA would have a continuing role, specifically that it would fund it and contribute the Chair and six committee members. But the constitution referred to the MCRA as the rural community council, an indication of the degree to which the MCRA's two roles were indistinguishable, even to those closely involved with the Association.
[13] MCRA, Secretary's report, 31 March 1951.
[14] MCRA, Articles of Association and Memorandum, 1950.
[15] See Appendix II.
[16] Jerman, 'The effects of the winds of change'.
[17] MCRA, minutes of council meeting, 18 September 1973.
[18] MCRA, secretary's report, October 1974.
[19] MCRA, minutes of council meeting, 4 February 1975.
[20] MCRA, minutes of council meeting, 29 April 1976.
[21] MCRA, minutes of council meeting, 18 September 1973 (Secretary's Report).
[22] MCRA, Pavilion correspondence, MCRA circular letter, 4 December 1971.

[23] MCRA, Pavilion correspondence, letter to *The Town Crier* (Newtown), MCRA chairman, 9 April 1974.
[24] MCRA, conveyance dated 29 March 1974.
[25] MCRA, Pavilion correspondence, letter to the Charity Commission, MCRA solicitors, 29 October 1973.
[26] MCRA, Pavilion correspondence, letter to the Charity Commission, MCRA secretary, 4 October 1978.
[27] MCRA, Pavilion correspondence, letter to the chairman of Montgomery District Council, the clerk of Newtown Town Council, 26 September 1978.
[28] MCRA, Pavilion correspondence, letter to the Charity Commission, MCRA solicitors 11 February 1980.
[29] MCRA, Pavilion correspondence, Draft Scheme, Charity Commission 1.4.1981
[30] MCRA, Pavilion correspondence, letters to MCRA secretary, MCRA solicitors, 15 November 1979; 15 December 1981.
[31] MCRA, Pavilion correspondence, letter to the MCRA solicitors, Charity Commission, 2 September 1981.
[32] MCRA, Minutes of council meeting, 16 July, 1982.
[33] MCRA, Minutes of Annual General Meeting, 1984.

6

[1] MCRA, Annual Report of the Powys Fine Art Committee, 1959.
[2] *Birmingham Daily Post*, 31 May 1965.
[3] MCRA, Minutes of the Powys Fine Art Committee, 11 December 1963.
[4] MCRA, Correspondence with the Hon. Camilla Davies 2019.
[5] MCRA, Minutes of MCRA Council, 10 June 1965.
[6] MCRA, The Gwendoline and Margaret Davies Memorial Gallery, souvenir brochure, 1967.
[7] *Birmingham Daily Post*, 19 June 1965.
[8] The lease was originally granted by Newtown and Llanllwchaiarn Urban District Council, whose interest was later transferred to Powys County Council. Rent was set at £1 per year for the duration of the lease.
[9] *Birmingham Daily Post*, 7 October 1967.
[10] MCRA, Minutes of the Annual General Meeting, 1969.
[11] National Library of Wales, Arts Council of Wales Records: Oriel 31 (Davies Gallery*)*. Submission document, Oriel 31, 16 October 1990.

[12] MCRA, Secretary's Report, January 1968. Sir Ben Bowen Thomas was chairman of the North Wales Arts' Association and president of the University College of Wales, Aberystwyth.
[13] MCRA, Secretary's Report, January 1968. The public meeting was held on 9 November 1967.
[14] MCRA, Secretary's Report, 1967.
[15] MCRA, Secretary's Report, 1967.
[16] MCRA, Secretary's Report, 1970.
[17] MCRA, Minutes of Annual General Meeting, 1984.
[18] MCRA, (Oriel file 6); letter to Montgomery District Council, 5 August 1985.
[19] MCRA, Minutes of MCRA Council, 28 October 1985.
[20] MCRA, Minutes of Annual General Meeting, 1986.
[21] MCRA, Annual Report, 1990.
[22] National Library of Wales, Arts Council of Wales Records: Oriel 31 (Davies Gallery*)*. Meeting note, unattributed, 16 October 1990.
[23] MCRA, Annual report, 1990.
[24] MCRA, Oriel file 6, Correspondence; Letter from Michael Nixon, 13 June1989.
[25] MCRA, Oriel files, Extension proposal from Oriel 31, 1990.
[26] National Library of Wales, Arts Council of Wales Records: Oriel 31 (Davies Gallery*),* 1991.
[27] National Library of Wales, Arts Council of Wales Records: Oriel 31 (Davies Gallery*))*. Handwritten note of a meeting between Oriel 31, Montgomery District Council and the County Council, unattributed, 16 October 1990.
[28] MCRA, Minutes of MCRA Council, 29 March, 1991.
[29] National Library of Wales, Arts Council of Wales Records: Oriel 31 (Davies Gallery*)*. Memorandum recording Oriel 31's expansion plans, Arts Council (Isabel Hitchman), 8 January 1993.
[30] National Library of Wales, Arts Council of Wales Records: Oriel 31 (Davies Gallery*)*. Memorandum recording Oriel 31's expansion plans, Arts Council (Isabel Hitchman), 8 January 1993.
[31] Michael Nixon, *'Creating Utopia?': New Architecture for the Arts* (Newtown, 1967), p. 67. Transcript of a conference held at the Regent Centre, Newtown, 31 May-1 June 1997.
[32] National Library of Wales, Arts Council of Wales Records: Oriel 31 (Davies Gallery). Memorandum 41.3(d), February 1993.
[33] National Library of Wales, Arts Council of Wales Records: Oriel 31 (Davies Gallery*),* Arts Council file note, unattributed, 16 October 1991; Memorandum 41.3, February 1993.
[34] National Library of Wales, G. G. Evans papers; minutes of MCRA Annual General Meeting, 17 January 1995.
[35] MCRA, Oriel files; notes of a meeting with Powys County Council, Llandrindod Wells; 12 March 1998.

[36] National Library of Wales, G. G. Evans papers; correspondence with Peter Dean, 22 February 1996.
[37] MCRA, Minutes of MCRA Council, 4 June 1996.
[38] MCRA, Minutes of MCRA Council, 4 June 1996.
[39] These consultants were Alex Gordon Tweedale. They were followed by Hugo Perks Associates.
[40] MCRA, Oriel file 4, Feasibility study, David Gomersall. The Davies *Charities* were later referred to as the Gwendoline and Margaret Davies *Charity*.
[41] MCRA, Press Cuttings, Shropshire Star, 4 April 1997. The full name of PAVO is the Powys Association of Voluntary Organisations.
[42] MCRA, Oriel file 2; Correspondence from Newtown Town Council, 31 July 1997.
[43] MCRA, Oriel file 5; Notes of meeting at County Hall, 12 March 1998.
[44] MCRA, Oriel file 3; Correspondence with Arts Council of Wales, 1 July 1998; quoted by Glyn Tegai Hughes, 1 July 1998
[45] MCRA, Oriel file 3; Correspondence with Arts Council of Wales, 1 July 1998; quoted by Glyn Tegai Hughes, 1 July 1998.
[46] MCRA, Oriel file 5/2. Memorandum GTH, 7 April 1998.
[47] MCRA, Minutes of MCRA Council, 30 November 1999.
[48] MCRA, Oriel files, Chadwick Jones Associates, undated.
[49] MCRA, Minutes of MCRA Council, 9 February 2000.
[50] MCRA, Minutes of MCRA Council, 4 December, 2000.
[51] MCRA, minutes of MCRA extraordinary meeting, 9 February 2000.
[52] MCRA, minutes of MCRA extraordinary meeting, 9 February 2000.
[53] MCRA, Oriel 31 Report, Chadwick Jones Associates. Undated.
[54] MCRA, Minutes of MCRA Council, 4 September 2000.
[55] MCRA, Annual Report, 2003.
[56] MCRA, Annual Report, 2005.
[57] MCRA, Annual Accounts and Directors Report, 2005.

Conclusions

[1] Correspondence with David Hall, 5 June 2019.

www.ingramcontent.com/pod-product-compliance
Lightning Source LLC
LaVergne TN
LVHW091213150826
845672LV00005B/1336

* 9 7 8 1 9 1 6 1 9 8 7 0 8 *